RASPBERRY PI

BEGINNER'S GUIDE TO LEARN THE REALMS OF RASPBERRY PI A-Z

≥ ROB STEPHEN ≤

Table of Contents

Introduction

This beginner-level book contains proven steps and strategies on how to use a Raspberry Pi.

Starting with the absolute basics, we'll gradually move to important concepts that a novice can easily digest. This book has tried to accommodate every type of person who is interested in working with a Raspberry Pi, regardless if you have a tech background or not.

Once you understand and can identify the different hardware components on the Raspberry Pi's circuit board, you can gradually move towards learning how to program code on the Raspberry Pi using both the Native Scratch programming language and the widely popular Python programming language. We'll go on an interactive journey to explore the programming capabilities of the Raspberry Pi and have provided detailed interactive examples at the end of the programming chapters so that you can learn how to program projects in real-time. And don't miss the useful tips at the end of chapter, which can be very helpful for beginners.

Before ending our journey, we briefly delve into the world of physical computing using Raspberry Pi. You'll end the journey being more capable of designing and understanding practical projects using the Raspberry Pi and will be able to take actionable steps on your own.

Chapter 1

Introducing You To The World Of Raspberry Pi

WHAT IS A RASPBERRY PI?

If you take a look at the structure of the Raspberry Pi, the first thing you'll notice is how small it is. The size of a Raspberry Pi is similar to that of a typical credit card. This small form-factor of the Raspberry Pi is itself a characteristic feature of the device, although it may not look entirely like a final product straight out of the box.

When compared to the modern PC motherboards, the Raspberry Pi is a computer that has been made available to the general consumer in an extremely small form-factor, low price tag, and functionality, which you would normally expect from a full-sized Personal Computer. Owing to such characteristics, the Raspberry Pi is suitable for a wide range of purposes. Browsing the internet, playing modest video games, interacting with popular social media channels, the perfect system to learn programming and coding, all the way to using the Raspberry Pi in innovative and creative projects building devices such as retro emulator in variety of forms and controlling and handling complex circuits. The Raspberry Pi does not have one specific use, in reality, it's the complete opposite;

in the sense that the limitations of the Raspberry Pi are in actuality the limitations of one's imagination regarding the projects in which this device can be used.

Moreover, there's an entire Raspberry Pi community on the internet dedicated to helping out people in their queries regarding the device. Whether you bought your first Raspberry Pi and need help setting it up or if you're using a Raspberry Pi in a project, you will be surprised at how positively and quickly the community joins the discussion forums and give their suggestions and feedback to your questions.

The Raspberry Pi is a computational device based on single-board architecture. The single-board architecture is a design scheme for computers in which the entire system is situated on a single circuit board. Just as how the Raspberry Pi is based on the single-board architecture, it has also inherited the small form-factor of the design, which is similar to the dimensions of a credit card. However, it is important to keep the power and functionality of a computer separate from the size of its motherboard or circuit, because such parameters of a system are not dependent on how big of a circuit the system is situated upon. As such, the Raspberry Pi is capable of handling and performing all the tasks a Personal Computer would be able to do, but the speed at which the tasks are performed is another realm of the discussion by factoring in different parameters.

The birth of Raspberry Pi was inspired by the notion that fully functioning computers in a compact size made available to the general consumer at a plausible price would hold enough power as to not only facilitate the educational industry but also making computer technology easy to implement and customize in various projects (educational projects, DIY projects or any experiment that can use the prowess of the Raspberry Pi); in short, the prospects are virtually unlimited). The Raspberry Pi Foundations was established in 2012, and after a limited production of units, the beta testing became a huge success and today, Raspberry Pi is the leading device which has taken a strong foothold in various human interactive environments including homes, offices, smart factories, data centers, interactive classrooms and other such places which can take advantage of the features of a small hand-held computer.

Different Models of Raspberry Pi

Since the journey of Raspberry Pi began to invoke the innovation among young programmers, The Pi system has gone through a series of revisions up till now, and since 2012, a total of 11 models of the Raspberry Pi have been released, beginning from;

1. Raspberry Pi B   (2012)

2. Raspberry Pi A+   (2014)

3. Raspberry Pi   2   (2015)

4. Raspberry Pi Zero   (2015)

5. Raspberry Pi 3   (2016)

6. Raspberry Pi Zero W   (2017)

7. Raspberry Pi Zero WH   (2018)

8. Raspberry Pi   3B+   (2018)

9. Raspberry Pi 3 Model A+   (2018)

10. Raspberry Pi 4 B   (2019)

Since the release of the first Raspberry Pi Model B, many models have followed each of which bringing in improved functionality and better specifications in general. Hence before you go out and get yourself a Raspberry Pi, be sure that you know which model you are purchasing and whether if it suits your needs.

Despite the changes made in every model of the Raspberry Pi, there remains one aspect which has not been changed from the original Raspberry Pi B, and that is the software compatibility. This means that the software running on the original Raspberry Pi is the same software that's being used by the latter versions; besides, the software being used in one Raspberry Pi is compatible with all other models, regardless if they're new or old. This is why the Raspberry Pi is so practical because it focuses on usability and functionality rather than marketing.

Just as how software developed for one Raspberry Pi model is compatible with the rest of the other models. Similarly, all the different concepts and functions that we will learn in this book can be applied to any model in the Raspberry Pi family. Hence, it won't make much of a difference for whatever Raspberry Pi model you own, but for this book, the model which we will consider to standardize our references will be the Raspberry Pi 4 Model B, the latest and most powerful single-board computer made up to this date.

THE ESSENTIAL COMPONENTS OF THE RASPBERRY PI

Before we talk about the components of the Raspberry Pi, let's discuss the structure of this device.

When taking an overview, the first thing that we notice is the naked layout or structure of the Raspberry Pi. This layout of a computer is unconventional and very different from the traditional layout of a typical computer, which has all of its components covered. But do not be confused as it is not necessary to have the Raspberry Pi exposed at all times. This opened structure is adopted because it increases the customizability of the device by making it easier for consumers to design a case for the computer according to the purpose and needs of their project.

With the open structure of the Raspberry Pi, we can easily analyze and discuss the various peripherals and components and their respective purposes.

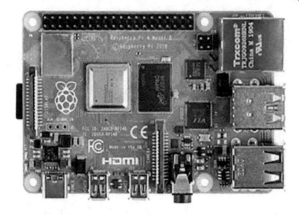

The Raspberry Pi 4 shown above is a Model B (4GB RAM). There's no need to panic after seeing all these components packed onto the tiny board. These components are very easy to understand, and besides, we are only going to discuss the main and essential components so that you are not overwhelmed.

THE SYSTEM-ON-CHIP (SOC)

A traditional computer can be seen to have many components, all of which are performing a specific task. However, to achieve uniformity in function and procedure to ultimately perform logical calculations and display useful information as output, a System-on-Chip is used as the main component to achieve this goal. This component not only coordinates all the parts of a system, but it also performs logical, arithmetic, and graphical operations.

Let's discuss what a System-on-Chip is without diving into too much technical detail. If you look at the above Raspberry Pi 4 model, you'll see a small square metal cap, just above the center of the board. This metal cap is a cover which houses the SoC. A System-on-Chip is a silicon chip which is installed on the integrated circuit of the board. This silicon chip is further made up of two components, ones that you might be familiar with;

- The CPU (Central Processing Unit)

- The GPU (Graphics Processing Unit)

The CPU handles the arithmetic and logic operations along with controlling the flow of information from the other components of the computer system.

On the other hand, the GPU is mainly involved in handling and processing visual (graphical) information, basically handling geometrical and physics calculations.

These two components combined become the Brain of the system.

RANDOM ACCESS MEMORY

As we have established that the SoC of the Raspberry Pi is the brain of the system, we can also relate it to the fact that a brain is handicapped without memory, it's useless. Similarly, the brain of the Raspberry Pi system also needs ample memory to function properly. For this purpose, the system has another chip located just below the SoC, and this black chip is known as the RAM (Random Access Memory) of the system.

A RAM is basically a component that provides high-speed temporary storage to the CPU. This serves the purpose of allowing your Raspberry Pi system to hold onto the unsaved information that you're working with until you save it. Only then will the information be written onto the permanent storage, in this case, the MicroSD card.

These two types of storages work together and can be classified as volatile and non-volatile storages.

The RAM is classified as volatile storage because the information is held within the RAM is lost as soon as the power is turned off.

The MicroSD card is classified as non-volatile storage because the information in this storage is not lost when the power is turned off; instead, the SD card holds the information until it is either corrupted or deleted.

THE WIRELESS CONNECTOR MODULE

To send and receive data wirelessly, the system needs to have a module that allows for the communication between devices. That's the job of the wireless connector module. It allows the Raspberry Pi to be able to communicate with computer networks, wireless peripherals, smart sensors, and smartphones.

The wireless module is located at the top right of the circuit board. A metallic lid covers the module.

The wireless connector module has two more components which are;

- The Wi-Fi radio

- The Bluetooth radio

The functions of these two components have already been briefly mentioned above, but to clarify the purpose of these components further, we will discuss their functions.

The Wi-Fi radio (transmitter and receiver module) allows the system to connect to the internet, a computer system, or a Wi-Fi-enabled network system.

The Bluetooth radio (transmitter and receiver module) hand allows the system to connect to other Bluetooth enabled devices (mainly peripherals, such as a keyboard, mouse, headphones or earphones, etc.). It also allows for the sending or receiving data from smart devices and smartphones close and range.

THE USB CONTROLLER

This is another essential component of the system. This module identifies Universal Serial Bus devices when connected via the port and relays the information to the main CPU.

What you need to know about the USB controller component is that it simply controls and runs the four USB ports. You can see the USB controller on the Raspberry Pi circuit as a plastic-covered black chip located at the bottom edge of the circuit board, just behind the middle set of USB ports.

You can plug in flash drives, USB keyboards, and mice or even connect smartphones via USB cables.

THE NETWORK CONTROLLER

The network controller is a comparatively smaller chip than the other components and is located right next to the USB controller chip.

Just as the name suggests, the network controller handles the receiving and sending of online network information via the Ethernet port.

This chip allows the Raspberry Pi to connect to the internet via a cable.

POWER MANAGEMENT INTEGRATED CIRCUIT (PMIC)

This power managing component is located to the upper left of the circuit board, just above the USB Type-C power connector. This component is a black chip that is visually smaller than the rest of the components mentioned so far.

This chip is commonly known as the Power Management Integrated Circuit because it handles the power distribution throughout the circuit, mainly redirecting the power coming in from the micro USB port to run the Raspberry Pi.

Remember, there's no need to memorize or cram the functions and locations of all these components. This is just to make you familiar with what each component's job is and where can you see it on the Raspberry Pi. If it's a lot to take in, relax and wait until you reach the end of this guide, by then, you'll become familiar with these components on your own.

DIFFERENT PORTS IN THE RASPBERRY PI AND THEIR USES

Like any full-sized computer, you'll find that the Raspberry Pi has all the necessary and essential ports within its tiny credit-card-sized circuit board.

THE USB PORTS

The USB ports are located to the right side of the Raspberry Pi's Processor chip and just beside the Ethernet port. The USB port is essential in any system, and in the Raspberry Pi, you'll notice that there are two sets of USB ports. These 4 USB ports provide ample connection space to plug in an external USB mouse, keyboard, a flash drive, a digital camera, or any USB supported peripheral.

If you look closely at these two sets of USB ports, you'll see that these ports have a color scheme different from the other set. One's interior is color-coded black while the other is color-coded blue. This is to indicate that these USB ports are a different version from each other. The black USB ports are based on the USB 2.0 version, while the blue USB ports are the newer USB 3.0 version, which is relatively faster than their predecessor.

THE ETHERNET PORT

The Ethernet port is located just beside the USB ports. This port is also commonly known as the network port because the purpose of this port is to enable the Raspberry Pi to be connected to the World Wide Web (Internet) through a wired connection.

To use the Ethernet port, you require an RJ45 connector cable that fits into the port. If you take a closer look at the Ethernet port, you'll notice that there are two very small LEDs at the bottom of the port's entrance. These LEDs actually serve the purpose of an indicator telling the user if the connection is working or not. We can also term these as the Status LEDs because they basically reflect the working status of the Ethernet port.

THE HEADPHONE JACK

Contrary to the trend of removing the headphone jack from popular smartphone devices and relying completely on Bluetooth connection for audio playback, the Raspberry Pi still houses the traditional 3.5mm headphone jack, technically termed as an Audio-Visual (AV) jack.

This is because the Raspberry Pi's Bluetooth connection is more likely to be connected to some other wireless peripherals such as a mouse, keyboard, or any other Bluetooth supported peripheral and hence having a dedicated physical audio port really helps. Moreover, being a port dedicating to outputting sound, this jack tends to reproduce better and crispier sound frequency, especially on amplified speakers.

Apart from reproducing sound, we have mentioned that this port is known as the *Audio-Visual jack.* Just as the name suggests, this port is also capable of carrying video signals across the Raspberry Pi towards output systems which support composite video signals, such as a TV or a Projector. However, to connect the Raspberry Pi to such devices, you would require an additional cable adapter, the TRRS (tip-ring-ring-sleeve).

The Audio jack is located just above the Ethernet port, and you can identify the port by its traditional 3.5mm size and round shape.

THE CAMERA CONNECTOR

This port is located just above the Headphone jack. It has a characteristic plastic flap that can be opened or closed, revealing the underlying camera connector. This connector is technically known as the Camera Serial Interface (CSI), allowing the user to have access to the specially designed camera interface of the Raspberry Pi. We will learn more about its uses in future chapters.

MICRO-HDMI PORTS

Apart from the AV jacks being able to carry video signals, there is another set of ports that are capable of performing the same task with better efficiency and quality. This set of ports is known as the micro High Definition Multimedia Interface, hence the name micro-HDMI.

You must have heard about HDMI because it's the most popular connector port being used in LEDs, consoles, graphic cards, and almost any device which has the capability of carrying video signals. The Raspberry Pi also kept up with the trends, but with a slight alteration; to accommodate two display ports on its small form-factor, the Raspberry Pi features a smaller version of the popular HDMI port but has functionality on par with the full-sized HDMI ports. That explains the "micro" part of this port, moving on to the "High Definition Multimedia Interface" this infers that the micro-HDMI port carries both audio and video signals with high-definition quality. As the Raspberry Pi has two micro-HDMI ports instead of one, you can connect it to one or two displays simultaneously.

The micro-HDMI ports are located towards the left-hand side edge of the circuit board. You'll see that just above these ports, there is a big white "HDMI" label written on the board itself.

USB TYPE-C POWER PORT

If you look just next to the micro-HDMI ports, you'll find a very familiar-looking port; this is a USB Type-C Port. This is a connector that acts as a bridge connection between the power source and the Raspberry Pi, ultimately powering up the whole system.

This specific choice of a power port makes the Raspberry Pi even more functionally diverse in its potential uses because Type C ports are now the trending USB ports in smartphones, tablets, and various other portable devices. You can also use a standard mobile charger with the Raspberry Pi, but it is highly recommended that you use the dedicated Type-C power port to power the device.

DISPLAY CONNECTOR

This is a really tricky connector port to sort through. At first glance, this connector seems identical to the camera connector, mentioned previously. Apart from its strange-looking shape and confusingly identical design to the camera connector, this port is actually the polar opposite; it is a Display Serial Interface (DSI) or a Display connector.

You must be wondering why there is a need for a display connector when we already have the Audio-Visual Jack and two micro-HDMI. Well, to answer this, we first need to explore what is the function of this connector. The main purpose and function of the

Display Serial Interface are to enable the user to have access to the touch display feature of the Raspberry Pi. Now, the AV jack and micro-HDMI ports only output and carry video along with audio signals, while the Display Serial Interface is designed for use with the Raspberry Pi touch display.

THE GPIO HEADER

This port is known as the General Purpose Input/Output header of the Raspberry Pi. The major function of this connector is to enable the Raspberry Pi to communicate with external hardware. This hardware can be as simple as LEDs and buttons to more complex hardware such as temperature sensors, joysticks, and pulse rate monitors.

The GPIO header is characterized by its 40 metal pins, which are further split into two rows of 20 metal pins. The header is located to the right-hand edge of the circuit board, just beside the System-on-Chip.

Apart from the GPIO header, there is another small four-pin header, which is very interesting. This header is basically involved in providing the Raspberry Pi power through a Power over Ethernet (PoE) HAT. The power is pulled in from the network connection instead of the USB Type-C Power port.

MICRO-SD CARD PORT

The Micro SD Card port is essentially the permanent storage of the Raspberry Pi. This SD card is capable of containing all of your personal files, installed software, along with the Operating System that will operate the whole Raspberry Pi. The Raspberry Pi OS is flashed to the Micro-SD card through a PC or a Laptop and then inserted into this Port.

You might have trouble finding the Micro SD Card port, and that's because this port is located to the opposite side of all the other connectors, the bottom side. If you flip the Raspberry Pi over, you'll see the Micro SD card port, which is beneath the Display connector.

RASPBERRY PI'S ESSENTIAL PERIPHERALS

Just as how any computer requires external peripherals to be able to interact with the user. The Raspberry also needs peripherals so that it can be classified as a computer system. Without peripherals, a computer is nothing more than a door-stop, similar is the case for a Raspberry Pi. The most minimum necessary and essential peripherals to be able to interact with the Raspberry Pi system are;

- A Micro-SD card

- A Display Output (LED, Monitor, TV)

- Input Devices (Keyboard and Mouse)

- 5V USB Type-C Power Supply at 3 Amps or higher

With these peripherals, we now have a fully functional computer system. The Micro SD card acts as our permanent storage device on which we load our Operating System and additional software along with our personal files.

The Display output can be any supported LED, monitor, or a TV so that the user can see what he's doing and extract visual information as the system's output.

The Input devices include both keyboards and mouse so that the user can instruct the Raspberry Pi with instructions and make the system perform actions.

And finally, a power supply with the above-specified voltage and current ratings so that you're system is supplied with ample power to function properly.

As we have mentioned clearly that the above peripherals are the bare minimum for the Raspberry Pi to function as a computer system, we can add-on more peripherals according to our needs. Some official Raspberry Pi peripherals recommended to be used with the system include;

- **A Raspberry Pi Case:** this case can be used to cover and protect the Raspberry Pi system whilst having access to all the important ports.

- **A Raspberry Pi Camera Module**

- **A Raspberry Pi Touch Display**: This add-on can be used to connect the Raspberry Pi to an external tablet-style screen providing both a video display output and a touchscreen interface

- **A Sense HAT:** this is an add-on with multiple uses and functions while being mainly used for physical computing.

The reason why the Raspberry Pi is a device that enables a person to tap into his imaginations and creativity to build an innovative project perforated with computational capabilities is that there is a wide array of third party accessories available to be used with the Raspberry Pi. You can design your own accessories through 3D printing or go through the huge assortment of 3rd party accessories looking for the perfect peripheral, add-on, or an accessory for your Raspberry Pi project. These varieties of accessories and kits can range from being able to turn your Raspberry Pi into a laptop or a tablet to giving the Pi the capability and functionality to understand human speech and talking back to the user. While this may encourage you to rush towards your nearest computer hardware shop and fill your shopping cart with these amazing accessories, we must first learn how to walk alongside the Raspberry Pi before running alongside it on a marathon.

GENERAL TIPS

- Although an external case is not necessary for the Raspberry Pi, it is recommended to get one so you can prevent the sensitive components of the system from accidental spillage of soda, water or any other liquid.

- When looking for an SD card to use as storage for your Raspberry Pi, take into consideration the project for which this system will be used and purchase a card with ample storage so you won't have to face storage issues during your Raspberry Pi project.

- It's recommended that you purchase a High-Speed Micro SD with recognized quality, preferably from known brands such as Samsung, Sony, and Kingston (there are many others, but we cannot mention all of them). Do not go for a cheap MicroSD alternative because they are more prone to data corruption and have a lower life-span.

- When purchasing accessories, also go for a suitable heat-sink if the Raspberry Pi project you're working on is demanding.

- Always get a dedicated and suitable power supply if you're planning to use the Raspberry Pi as your daily driver for a computer system. Low capacity power supplies can damage the system when additional or demanding peripherals or accessories are attached.

Chapter 2

Setting Up Your Raspberry Pi

In this chapter, we will learn how we can use the essential peripherals, mentioned in the previous chapter, to set up our Raspberry Pi. We will also discover some essential items that our Raspberry Pi will require and how to connect all of them to get it set up and working in no time.

SETTING UP THE HARDWARE

ASSESSING WHAT YOU HAVE AND REQUIRE

Although the Raspberry Pi is designed in such a way to allow anybody to easily and quickly set it up and have it running from the get-go. However, just as how any computer requires external components so that the user can interact with the system, the Raspberry Pi is no exception. It also requires proper peripherals to start functioning as a computer system, although it has been designed easy to set up, the need to set it up remains.

Hence, the first thing you should do after purchasing a Raspberry Pi is to take a look at what peripherals do you have that you can use with the system. Normally, with the purchase of a Pi system, a starter kit is also included so that the user can immediately set it up.

However, in the case where you do not have a starter kit, you'll need to arrange the following peripherals to set up the Raspberry Pi system;

The USB Type C Power Supply

As mentioned in the previous chapter, you first need a power source so that you can turn on the Pi system. According to the rapidly shifting power demands of the Raspberry Pi, it's recommended to get the official Raspberry Pi Power Supply, which has been engineered specifically for the system. The alternative to the official power supply is the 5V power supply rated at three amps or higher with a USB Type-C connector. Before plugging the power supply into the Type-C power port of the Raspberry Pi, proceed to plug in all the other peripherals.

MicroSD Card

Just as how a computer system requires a permanent storage solution, typically an HDD or SSD, the Raspberry Pi system also needs a storage solution. In this case, we use a MicroSD card and put it in the MicroSD port. Before using the MicroSD card with the Pi system, you should flash the card with the Raspbian Operating System. An alternative to flashing an OS onto a card is to get one pre-installed with the New-Out-Of-The-Box-Software (NOOBS). It is recommended to get a 128 GB card so that the system has room to grow, and you won't have to go rummaging through shops for a new MicroSD card when you're running out of storage space on the Pi System. After installing the required OS software onto the card, pop it into the MicroSD Card Port.

USB Keyboard and Mouse

This one is a no brainer unless you have a Display connector set up with a touch screen interface, you will need these input peripherals to communicate with the system. Get a USB keyboard according to your preferences and a mouse that fits your hand comfortably. Plug these peripherals into the USB 2.0 ports, and you are now ready to interact with your Pi System, but there's still one more peripheral we're missing, and that's the display peripheral.

Micro-HDMI Cable

The last and equally important peripheral that you need to set up your Pi system initially is the Micro-HDMI cable so that you can plug in your Raspberry Pi to an LED, Monitor, or TV that has HDMI support. While getting a Micro-HDMI cable, keep in mind the length of the cable, you don't want it to be so lengthy that it would cause problems in cable management and you don't want it to be so short that the cable won't even reach to the display device. If you're using an older display device, you can also get HDMI to DVI-D, DisplayPort, or VGA adapters to connect your Raspberry Pi with such old display devices.   After you've bought the micro-HDMI cable, connect it to your display, and you're now ready to go.

PROCEEDING TO SET UP THE HARDWARE

Now that we have organized all of the peripherals needed to turn the Raspberry Pi into a fully functional device, we can finally proceed to set up the hardware of the device.

Before we dive right into setting up the Pi system, we first need to address the fact that the Raspberry Pi is a durable piece of technology, not indestructible. Hence, whenever handling the Pi manually, always be sure to hold the Raspberry Pi board by the edges instead of holding it by the flat sides. Making this practice into a habit actually prevents any accidental bending of raised metal pins at the bottom. This can cause various complications if they do become bent, either by careless handling or by putting too much force on the bottom side of the Raspberry Pi's circuit board.

Let's get into setting up the hardware for the Pi!

INSTALLING THE RASPBERRY PI INTO A CASING (OPTIONAL)

Assembling the case and installing the Raspberry Pi system onto it is an optional step as you can choose to work with the Raspberry Pi with our without the case. However, it's strongly recommended that you choose a suitable casing for the Pi system as you cannot leave the circuit board laying out in the open, making the circuitry of the system extremely vulnerable to humidity and accidental spillage.

You can make or order a custom Raspberry Pi casing or use the Official Raspberry Pi case. As we will be mostly using official Raspberry Pi hardware as they are easily available and accessible, we will consider the official Raspberry Pi case for demonstrative purposes.

Now, take out the official Raspberry Pi case and split the case into individual pieces, the red base, and the white lid. Follow the steps detailed below;

- Hold the red base in such a way that the flat part of the base is to your right, and the raised end of the base is to the left away from you.

- You will observe that there are slots made on the side of the case specifically for the connector ports of the Pi. Without inserting the MicroSD card yet, pick up the Raspberry Pi board and place it inside the red base casing in such a way that the USB Type C, Micro HDMI, and the 3.5mm audio ports fit perfectly into their respective holes and the USB and Ethernet ports are towards to the flat end of the casing's base.

- Now, pick up the white lid of the casing and correctly align it to the red base, matching the layout. Push the lid in, enclosing the circuit board until you hear a satisfying click. You have now successfully installed the Raspberry Pi into a casing.

INSTALLING THE MICRO SD CARD INTO THE SYSTEM

After you have encased the Raspberry Pi system, flip the casing over so that you can see the backside. You will now see a labeled slot for the MicroSD card insertion. Slide the MicroSD card into the slot until it stops following an audible click sound, indicating the card has been successfully inserted.

Removing the card from the system is also very straightforward. Just as how we inserted the SD card into the slot without pushing it with too much pressure, similarly, just grip onto the end of the micro SD card protruding out and pull on it gently till it comes out. Older versions of the Raspberry Pi require you first to push it slightly then pull it out, but on the Models 3 and 4, there's no need to do this.

CONNECT THE KEYBOARD AND MOUSE

The next step toward setting up your Raspberry Pi is connecting your input devices, i.e., a keyboard and a mouse to the system. You have liberty to connect your USB peripherals to either the 2.0 ports or the 3.0 ports, but it is recommended to connect the keyboard and mouse to a 2.0 port as the USB port's version does not affect these two peripherals in any way, so if you use a 3.0 port or a 2.0 port for a keyboard or a mouse, it won't make a difference. So you should leave the 3.0 USB port for your flash drives or other peripherals that support USB 3.0 as this allows the devices mentioned above to work even faster in contrast to when they are connected to a USB 2.0 port.

The USB ports are right next to the Ethernet port, pick up the USB cable of the keyboard and mouse and plug it into the USB ports. Now you've set up the input devices you'll need to operate your Raspberry Pi system.

CONNECTING THE RASPBERRY PI TO A DISPLAY

For connecting the Raspberry Pi to a display, you have multiple options; Using the Display Serial Interface (Connecting to a TouchScreen display), Using the A/V jack, or using the Micro-HDMI connection.

The recommended option is the Micro-HDMI connection. To set up a display, pick up the Micro-HDMI cable and connect the smaller end of the cable to the HDMI port in your Raspberry Pi and plug the other end of the cable into your HDMI-supported display. One thing to note when plugging into the HDMI port of a TV or display is that check whether the display has more than one HDMI ports if so, take notice of the port's number written beside it as you'll need to switch the TV or display to this input to see the Pi's display. If there's no port number specified, just surf through each display option, and you'll eventually land on the correct one.

CONNECTING A NETWORK CABLE TO THE PI SYSTEM (OPTIONAL)

This step is optional because it depends on your preference, whether you wish to connect the Raspberry Pi to the internet using a wired connection (via the Ethernet Port) or by using a wireless connection (Using the Pi's integrated Wi-Fi module).

To connect the Raspberry Pi to a wired network, you need to take the Ethernet cable connected to the internet router, network hub, or a network switch and push it into the Raspberry Pi's Ethernet port with the plastic clip facing forwards until you hear an audible click. Before removing the Ethernet cable, you need to squeeze the plastic clip inwards and then slide the cable outwards.

CONNECTING A POWER SUPPLY TO THE SYSTEM

After we have connected all the other peripherals and hardware into the respective ports of the Raspberry Pi, all that's stopping us from turning the system on is a power supply, and this last step in the hardware setup process should always be performed only when you are ready to set up the software of the Pi system. This is because the Raspberry Pi does not include a power switch and turns on as soon as it is connected to a power supply. Therefore, you need to be ready to operate the Raspberry Pi before plugging in the power supply.

First, connect the USB Type-C end of the power supply cable to the USB Type-C power connector on the Raspberry Pi. It can go in either way around and should slide home gently. If your power supply has a detachable cable, make sure the other end is plugged into the body of the power supply.

Now, take the power supply connected to the Raspberry Pi and plug it into the mains power socket and turn the switch socket on; you'll observe that the display lights up, and the Raspberry Pi starts running. We have now completely set up the hardware of our Raspberry Pi, and now we are ready to dive in and set up the software of the Raspberry Pi.

SETTING UP THE SOFTWARE

Before we can proceed to use the Raspberry Pi as a fully functional computer system, we first need to install and set-up a proper system software, the Operating System.

As we have mentioned in the previous chapter that users can either flash the SD card with the Raspberry Pi official OS, the Raspbian, or by getting a microSD card with a NOOBS software pre-loaded onto it. Flashing the SD card with an OS is a complicated procedure, and hence, we will skip it and demonstrate how to set up the system software using the NOOBS tool. This software tool is specifically designed to make the overall procedure of setting up a software simple, easy, clean and fast by presenting the user with several options between different operating systems to choose from and install the selected OS automatically. You can do all of this in a little more than a few clicks of your mouse

When you first boot up a new Raspberry Pi system with a microSD card that has a fresh installation of NOOBS on it, then you will be prompted with a menu screen.

This is a NOOBS boot menu without any Operating System installed onto the Pi system. This menu allows you the capability of choosing any of the Operating Systems listed on it. In this NOOBS menu, there are two standard Operating Systems included, which require no downloading, you can select and install them right away. These Operating Systems are;

- The Recommended Raspbian OS; This is a custom version of the Debian Linux which has been tailored and optimized specifically for the Raspberry Pi system

- The LibreELEC OS; This is basically a variant/version of the Kodi Entertainment Center Software.

Moreover, if your Raspberry Pi has access to the internet via a wired or wireless connection (Accessed through the Wifi Networks 'w' option from the top bar of icons), you have the option to download and install other operating systems of your choice, but it is recommended that you stick to Raspbian as it is a custom-made software for Raspberry Pi.

We will now proceed to install the Raspbian OS. To do this, all you need to do is check the small box beside the Raspbtian icon, and you'll notice that the "install (i)" menu icon is no longer greyed out, this means that your selected operating system is now ready to be installed. So we will go ahead and click the 'install (i)' icon so that the software beings the installation procedure. You'll also be prompted with a message box saying that installing the operating system will overwrite any existing data stored on the microSD card. This warning message is of no concern to us because firstly, we are using a clean NOOBS microSD card, so we don't have any data that we would want to keep. Secondly, the installation procedure does not overwrite or delete NOOBS itself, so we will quickly press the "Yes" button and let the installation procedure begin.

The installation procedures vary from system to system (of the same model) because the installation time depends on how fast is the microSD card that you're using. The average installation can take anywhere from 10 minutes to 30 minutes to complete, so sit back and watch a few cat videos on your cell phone while the installation is finished.

When the installation is finished, a window will pop up with an 'OK' button; this is basically asking you to restart the system. Click the OK button, and the system will exit the NOOBS menu and reboot into the freshly installed Operating System. The first time the Raspberry Pi boots into an OS, it can take a few minutes to bring you to the desktop because the system is adjusting itself to effectively and efficiently make the best use of the free space on your microSD card. The next bootup will be much faster, as everything will be in order by then.

When the system successfully boots up, you'll be taken to the desktop of the Raspbian OS. Over here, you'll briefly see a window with the Raspberry Pi logo displayed on it just before the Raspbian desktop and setup wizard appears.

Finally, your Raspberry Pi's Operating System software has been successfully installed and is ready to be configured.

GENERAL TIPS

1. If your TV or monitor doesn't have an HDMI connector, that doesn't mean you can't use the Raspberry Pi. Adapter cables, available from any electronics stockist, will allow you to convert the micro-HDMI port on the Raspberry Pi to DVI-D, DisplayPort, or VGA for use with older computer monitors; these are simply connected to the Pi's micro-HDMI port, then a suitable cable used to connect the adapter cable to the monitor. If your TV has only a composite video or SCART input, you can purchase 3.5 mm tip-ring-ring-sleeve (TRRS) adapter cables and composite-to-SCART adapters that connect to the 3.5 mm AV jack.

2. If you can't see the Raspberry Pi on your display, check you are using the correct input. If your TV or monitor has more

than one HDMI input, switch through each, in turn, using the 'Source' or 'Input' button until you see the NOOBS menu

3. Make sure that the Operating System installation isn't interrupted as this has a high likelihood of damaging the software, a process known as data corruption. Do not remove the microSD card or unplug the power cable while the operating system is being installed; if something does happen to interrupt the installation, unplug the Pi from its power supply, then hold down the SHIFT key on the keyboard as you connect the Raspberry Pi back up to its power supply to bring the NOOBS menu back up. This is known as recovery mode and is a great way to restore a Pi whose software has been corrupted to working order again. It also allows you to enter the NOOBS menu after a successful installation, to reinstall the operating system, or install one of the other operating systems.

Chapter 3

Learning To Use Your Raspberry Pi

You have probably used personal computers, laptops, or smart-tablets. These devices also use Operating System software, namely Microsoft Windows, Mac OS, or Linux. If you are familiar with the look and feel of the windows, icons, menus, and pointers of these Operating System software, then you will quickly get used to the Raspbian OS as it features similar design principles of this popular OS software.

In the previous chapters, we talked about the different hardware components of a Raspberry Pi system and how to set up the hardware. In this chapter, we will take it a step further and learn how to use the Raspberry Pi system by understanding the Raspbian Operating System.

We will cover the first setup wizard you will encounter with the major pre-installed software loaded onto the device.

THE WELCOME WIZARD

As soon as you start up your Raspberry Pi after a fresh installation of the Raspbian OS, you'll encounter a first-time setup wizard. This is actually a really helpful tool that walks you through calibrating your Raspberry Pi system and allowing you to personalize some settings. This procedure is also known as the "configuration" of your Pi system.

1. As you progress through the setup procedure by clicking the 'Next' button, you'll be prompted to specify your country, preferred language, and timezone. This helps the system to use the appropriate dictionary for your selected language, and characters on the screen are displayed in the language you selected. Once you set the timezone, the system will automatically update the date and time accordingly. If you look just below these drop-down lists, you'll see a box that specifies the "Use US keyboard" option. This option is for cases where you have been using the US-layout keyboard regardless of the language you selected. Make sure Raspbian uses the correct keyboard layout. The other option, "Use English language," basically sets the default language of the desktop and programs to be English regardless of the native language you have specified above.

2. After finishing setting up the country, language, and timezone, proceed by clicking next. This will take you to the next window prompting you to set up a password for your user account to prevent unauthorized login to your Raspberry Pi system.

3. When you have finished setting up a strong password, the configuration wizard will display a list of available Wi-Fi connections near you and ask you to connect to one. If you

are planning to use a wired (Ethernet) connection instead of a wireless connection, then you can simply skip this part of the setup by clicking the 'Skip' button.

4. The version of OS installed from the NOOBS menu doesn't need to be up-to-date. If you have an older NOOBS version, then the OS will obviously not include its newer firmware updates. Hence, this configuration wizard gives you the option to check for system updates and install them if you are indeed running an older version of the OS. This is not a necessary step, but it is recommended to go through a system update check regardless because Raspbian is regularly updated to patch out and fix some system bugs, add new features to the OS and improve system performance through optimization. Downloading the system update can take some time based on how fast is your internet connection. When the updates have been downloaded and successfully installed, the system will display a window with the message 'System is up to date,' click the OK button and continue through the configuration.

5. This is the final screen of the setup wizard and prompts the user that, to wrap up and apply the specified configuration, the system requires a reboot. You can restart the system immediately or click the 'Later' button to delay the system reboot. Once you have restarted the system and logged into the desktop by entering your password, you will not be prompted with the welcome wizard again, and the settings

specified earlier will have been saved and applied to the system. Now Pi's software is ready to be explored.

NAVIGATING THROUGH THE DESKTOP INTERFACE

On the desktop interface, there are two icons placed by default, namely; The Wastebasket and the Removable drive. These are the same as the Recycle Bin and ThisPC icons found on Microsoft Windows desktops. At the top, you'll see the Raspbian OS taskbar, which allows the user to actually load programs that are then indicated as tasks in the taskbar.

Going to the right-hand side of the taskbar, you will find familiar icons, each representing features commonly found in every smart-device nowadays. From left to right, we have;

- The Media Eject icon

- The Bluetooth icon

- The Network icon

- The Volume icon

- The Clock icon

Going through the features of each of these icons chronologically, if you have a removable storage media connected to the Pi system, such as a USB flash drive, the Media Eject icon will display a selection of options, the main one being the Safely eject and remove media storage.

Besides the Media eject icon, you'll find the Network icon. This icon will change depending on the type of connection you're using. If you are connected to a wireless network, then you'll see a series of bars indicating the strength of the signal, and if you're connected to a wired network, you will just see two arrows. Clicking on the network icon will open up a drop-down menu showcasing all the available wireless connections and Turn Off Wi-Fi options.

Moving onwards is the Bluetooth icon; this icon will help you connect and pair with another Bluetooth device such as wireless peripherals and devices.

The volume icon opens the volume mixer and gives access to the sound control panel while the Clock icon displays a calendar and gives access to date and time options.

Going to the opposite side, the left-hand side of the taskbar, you will find some useful launcher icons which give the user access to some commonly used features of the Raspberry Pi. From right to left, we have;

- The Command Prompt launcher

- The File Explorer launcher

- The Web Browser launcher

- The Menu launcher

The Menu launcher basically opens up a list showing where you'll find programs that are installed alongside Raspbian. Whenever you install a new program, it'll be added into its respective category into this menu launcher from where you can quickly navigate and access the program. The other launchers are self-explanatory in their functions, the command prompt launcher opens up a Command Prompt where you can directly instruct the system to perform actions, the File Explorer launcher opens up an explorer in which you can go through the contents of your microSD card, and you can access the internet through the pre-installed Web Browser launcher. We will discuss the details of these programs in the next section.

THE CHROMIUM WEB BROWSER

If you've ever used Google Chrome, the Chromium Web Browser will feel incredibly similar and easy to use. To open the Chromium Web Browser, simply open the menu launcher and position the mouse pointer over the Internet category, related programs will be shown, and the Chromium Web Browser will be among them. Simply click it to open it up.

To start using Chromium, make sure that you are connected to a wireless or wired internet connection and type in any website that you know of to start things off. For example, a google search engine is a good place to be surfing the internet. You can also maximize the Chromium window so that it occupies the maximum screen space available.

The Chromium may also open up several web pages automatically on startup. These multiple web pages are displayed in separate tabs. To switch between web pages, you can click on the respective tab. You can also open a new tab by pressing the '+' icon beside an existing tab and also close an opened tab by pressing the 'x' on a tab.

THE FILE MANAGER (EXPLORER)

Another name for the File Explorer is the File Manager. It is common to refer to this program by a variety of names, the most common ones being those mentioned above.

In this program, you can explore and manage all of the files saved on to your storage media, regardless if they are files, programs, videos, images, web pages or games, you can access every file and manage them in the File Manager.

The major function of the File Manager is to give the user access to directories (organized files and folders). You can access directories both on your microSD card and on any removable storage media (such as a USB drive) that you connect your Raspberry Pi to. When you first open up the File Manager, the default window will be your home directory. In this directory, you'll find a series of sub-folders known as sub-directories, which are arranged in categories just like the items in the menu launcher. The main sub-directories are;

1. DESKTOP: This folder is what you see when you first load Raspbian; if you save a file in here, it will appear on the Raspbian desktop, making it easy to find and load.

2. DOCUMENTS: The Documents folder is home to most of the files you'll create, from short stories to recipes

3. DOWNLOADS: When you download a file from the internet using the Chromium web browser, it will be automatically saved in Downloads.

4. MUSIC: Any music you create or put on the Raspberry Pi can be stored here.

5. VIDEOS: A folder for videos, and the first place most video-playing programs will look.

6. PICTURES: This folder is specifically for pictures, known in technical terms as image files.

7. MAGPI: This folder contains an electronic copy of The MagPi, the official magazine of the Raspberry Pi Foundation.

8. PUBLIC: While most of your files are private, anything you put in Public will be available to other users of the Raspberry Pi, even if they have their own username and password.

Upon initial inspection, the File Manager is separated into two panes, an easy access pane which is the left pane that shows the directories on the Raspberry Pi and the explorer pane which is the right pane which shows the subdirectories and files of the directory which is selected in the left pane.

You can also copy, delete, cut, and modify folders and files through the File Manager. For example, as soon as you plug in a USB flash drive, a window will pop up asking if you want to display the contents of the removable drive in the File manager. Clicking on the Yes button will open up a separate window of the File manager which will display all the contents (files and folders) of the removable drive, you can now copy, cut, delete and edit these files and folders directly. Copying contents from removable drives such as these is also a very simple procedure, all you need to do is select the file or folder you want to copy, right-click it, a drop-down option will appear in which you can find the copy function. Click that, and the file has been copied on to the system's clipboard. Go to the directory where you want to copy the data and right-click on any empty space in the directory and click the paste function.

When you've finished experimenting, close the File Manager by clicking the close button at the top-left of the window. If you have more than one window open, close them all. If you have connected a removable storage device to your Pi, eject it by clicking the eject button at the top right of the screen, finding it in the list, and clicking on it before unplugging it.

THE LIBRE OFFICE PRODUCTIVITY SUITE

This piece of software is essentially the Raspberry Pi version of Microsoft Office Suite of applications. The LibreOffice contains all the necessary productivity tools, a word processor, a spreadsheet application, a Powerpoint application, etc.

To access the LibreOffice productivity suite, all you need to do is click on the Raspberry menu icon, move your mouse pointer to Office, and click on LibreOffice writer. This will only open up the word processor application from the LibreOffice productivity suite.

You can open other applications of the LibreOffice by exploring the Office category in the start menu.

The complete LibreOffice Productivity suite contains;

1. LibreOffice Base: This application is basically a tool for storing information, quickly navigating to the stored information, and analyzing it. In short, it's a database.

2. LibreOffice Calc: This application is similar to Microsoft Excel; it's a spreadsheet viewer and editor. This tool is essentially used for handling numbers, creating charts and graphs.

3. LibreOffice Draw: This program acts as a tool for users to be able to create pictures and diagrams; it's an illustration application.

4. LibreOffice Impress: This application is designed to be a tool allowing users to create slides and running slideshows. In other words, this is a presentation program.

5. LibreOffice Math: A formula editor, a tool for creating properly formatted mathematical formulae that can then be used in other documents.

LibreOffice is also available for other computers and operating systems. If you enjoy using it on your Raspberry Pi, you can download it for free from libreoffice.org and install it on any Microsoft Windows, Apple macOS, or Linux computer.

GENERAL TIPS

1. Built-in wireless networking is only available on the Raspberry Pi 3, Pi 4, and Pi Zero W families. If you want to use another model of Raspberry Pi with a wireless network, you'll need a USB WiFi adapter.

2. Closing a window before you've saved any work you've done is a bad idea; while many programs will warn you to save when you click the close button, others won't

3. When you see a keyboard shortcut like CTRL+C, it means to hold down the first key on the keyboard (CTRL), press the second key (C), then let go of both keys.

4. Always use the eject button before unplugging an external storage device; if you don't, the files on it can become corrupt and unusable.

5. Get in the habit of saving your work, even if you haven't finished it yet. It will save you a lot of trouble if there's a power cut, and you're interrupted part-way through.

6. Most programs include a Help menu, which has everything from information about what the program is to guides on how to use it. If you ever feel lost or overwhelmed by a program, look for the Help menu to reorient yourself.

7. Different countries have different rules about what frequencies a WiFi radio can use. Setting the WiFi country in the Raspberry Pi Configuration Tool to a different Country from the one you're actually in is likely to make it struggle to connect to your networks and can even be illegal under radio licensing laws – so don't do it!

8. Never pull the power cable from a Raspberry Pi without shutting it down first. Doing so is likely to corrupt the operating system and could also lose any files you have created or downloaded.

THE RECOMMENDED SOFTWARE TOOL

The Raspbian OS comes pre-loaded with a lot of useful applications such as the LibreOffice suite and chromium. However, this does not mean that the Raspbian OS does not support other 3rd party apps. On the contrary, the Raspbian is compatible with a wide range of applications, to browse such software, the Recommended Software Tool is there to help you.

By using this tool, you can go through an entire list filled with software which is compatible with the Raspbian OS. After finding an application that you want to install onto the system, all you need to do is double click the selected application or check the tick-box beside the application's icon, then click the install button manually.

The only pre-requisite of using the Recommended Software Tool is an internet connection because the tool requires active access to the web to retrieve the list of available software for the Raspbian OS to display it to the user and then to download the selected application directly.

This software tool also provides users the capability to choose an application and uninstall it. If you have downloaded an application, find that it's not how you thought it to be, simply right click that application and select remove. You can re-install the same application by just clicking the application's icon again and putting the tick back.

An additional tool for installing or uninstalling software, the Add/Remove Software tool, can be found in the same Preferences category of the Raspbian menu. This offers a wider selection of software, but which has not been vetted by the Raspberry Pi Foundation.

THE RASPBERRY PI CONFIGURATION TOOL

The configuration tool is an important program that gives you the flexibility to tweak and change the settings in the Raspbian OS. Most of the time, you will feel the need to access the settings of the Raspbian because the default settings are never the optimal settings. Every person has different preferences, so if you know your way around the settings, the configuration tool will help you access them and make the necessary changes.

To access the Configuration Tool, all you need to do is open the Raspberry menu, move the pointer of your mouse over to the Preferences category and then simply click on the Raspberry Pi Configuration Tool to load it up.

The first thing you will notice is that the Configuration has four separate tabs. Each tab controls a particular aspect of the Raspbian system. These four tabs are;

1. System: allows the user permission to change the password of the user account, set a hostname (this is the selected name

which the Raspberry Pi identifies itself by on local wireless and local wired networks) and displaying a range of some system settings which should only be played with if you know what you're doing. Otherwise, it is best to leave these settings alone.

2. Interface: these settings are disabled by default because they are associated with the new hardware, which is added to the Raspberry Pi system, for instance, a Raspberry Pi Camera Module.

3. Performance: this tab allows the user to configure the amount of memory used by the Raspberry Pi's graphical processing unit (GPU) and also to overclock the Pi's processor. Overclocking is basically increasing the processor's speed from the factory default speed. However, overclocking is should be done with proper instructions and guidance as it can damage your system's hardware because of over-heating.

4. Localization: here, you can change your locale, which controls things like the language used in Raspbian and how numbers are displayed, change the time zone, change the keyboard layout, and set your country for WiFi purposes.

SHUTTING DOWN THE RASPBERRY PI

The most important skill to learn when using a Raspberry Pi is to shut it down safely. The Raspberry Pi keeps all unsaved files in its volatile memory (memory which is emptied when the system is shut down), so you should develop the habit of shutting down the system safely, so you do not risk losing important data.

Click on the raspberry icon at the top left of the desktop and then click on Shutdown. A window will appear with three options; Shutdown, Reboot, and Logout.

The shutdown is the option you'll use most: clicking on this will tell Raspbian to close all open software and files, then shut the Pi down. Once the display has gone black, wait a few seconds until the flashing green light on the Pi goes off; then, it's safe to turn off the power supply.

The reboot is essentially the same as shutting down the system, but instead of completely turning the system off, the system goes through a procedure of automatically starting up as soon as it finishes shutting down. Installation of some applications may prompt a system reboot, hence you should properly restart the system instead of pulling out the power supply.

Logout is basically useful in scenarios where there are more than one user accounts created on the Raspberry Pi. To switch between user accounts or to turn off a user account without shutting down the system, you can choose the logout option. If you hit Logout by mistake and want to get back in, simply type 'pi' as the username and whatever password you chose in the Welcome Wizard at the start of this chapter.

Chapter 4

Starting From Scratch

In this chapter, we will learn to code by using Raspberry Pi's own block-based programming language – Scratch.

The Raspberry Pi provides the ideal environment for beginners and veteran coders alike to experiment and create original application software. So buckle up and be ready to explore your imagination to conjure ideas to incorporate into your coding project. Not only is this fun, it will also enable you to understand the Raspberry Pi better than before. Also, you will also be able to operate the Pi system not as a user but also as a developer and with time and experience, you will only get better.

The Pi system uses the "Scratch" programming language. The language was initially developed in the Massachusetts Institute of Technology (MIT) and later on, adopted by the Raspberry Pi as the key to the accessibility of coding on the Raspberry Pi.

The major difference between Scratch and other traditional programming languages is that Scratch is a **visual programming language** while others (Python, C++ and java, etc.) are **text-based**

programming languages. To further elaborate, Scratch allows you to build a program by using blocks (pre-written bundle of code) sequentially; in contrast, Python uses text-based lines of code to instruct the computer to carry out a task. This makes Scratch a lot easier and very user-friendly.

Although Scratch is very impactful in making coding easier for young and old users alike, however, this ease of usability does not mean that the coding language falls behind the traditional and commonly used programming languages. On the contrary, Scratch is just as powerful as these mainstream programming languages, and you can even create simple animations and games all the way to programming complex interactive robotics projects on your Raspberry Pi through Scratch.

INTRODUCTION TO THE SCRATCH INTERFACE

Before we proceed further, we need to address one main issue of Scratch in older Raspberry Pi models. Old models such as Pi Zero, Model A, A+, B, or B+ use an older version of Scratch, while the newer models use an updated version of Scratch, commonly known as Scratch 2, which is not compatible with old Raspberry Pi models (as mentioned previously). When learning about Scratch and its features, we will refer to the newer version.

With that out of the way, let's look at the Scratch 2 interface and describe it accordingly.

1. *THE STAGE*: The stage visually represents characters in your code. These characters move around the stage area

under the instructions detailed in your code. These characters who sit on the stage are also commonly referred to as sprites.

2. *THE MENU BAR*: This is just a typical menu bar, featuring a whole array of options giving you access to configure Scratch and change a few setting

3. *THE SPRITES PANE:* This pane displays all of the characters (sprites) that you have created or loaded so far. You can select a specific sprite you want to use in your project from this pane.

4. *BACKDROPS PANE:* This pane is also known as the stage controls because using this pane, you can change your stage or even add your own pictures as backgrounds if you so wish.

5. *BLOCKS PALETTE:* All the blocks available for your program appear in the blocks palette, which features color-coded categories.

6. *BACKPACK:* This is the area where you can see the blocks (pre-written chunks of code) of a specific category chosen in the blocks palette. You can select a block from the backup to build your program step-by-step.

7. *SCRIPTS AREA:* This is the area where you drag and drop the blocks from the backpack. You basically build the program by orderly dropping blocks into this area and then running the entire script once you have set the blocks in the proper order.

BUILDING YOUR VERY OWN SCRATCH PROGRAMMES

Just as any ordinary application on the Raspberry Pi, Scratch can be opened up by navigating to the Raspberry Pi menu and opening the Programming section on the list. Over there, you'll find Scratch 2 (assuming you are using the latest Pi model), click it and wait for the user interface to load up.

As discussed before, Scratch instructs the computer to perform a task by identifying code blocks used in the scripts by the user. Let's create a Scratch program, to do this, move your cursor over to the block palette and select the Looks category. You'll notice purple-colored blocks show up in the Backpack, in these numerous blocks, find the "Say Hello!" block and drag it to the Scripts area by right-clicking it, holding it and dragging it over to the Script then letting it go.

Once you've added the block to the Scripts area, the shape of the block will change. Now, the block has a hole at its top side and a matching part sticking out at the bottom, resembling that of a jigsaw piece. This infers that the block is capable of being attached to another block that can come before it or after it. When we add something to the top of this block, it will be known as a "trigger." This basically triggers the activation of the block below it. To understand it better, we will add a 'trigger' to the application we are currently working on. Go to the blocks palette and select the 'Events' category, bringing up brown colored blocks. These are mainly called 'hat blocks' because they are mostly used on the top side of other blocks.

Now from the backpack, select the 'when clicked' block and position it in the empty space on the top side of the purple block. No need to be accurate or precise in the positioning though, just bring it close enough, and it will automatically snap-in. We have now completed our first-ever Scratch program!

To check how our new program works, we need to run it. To run the program, all we have to do is to go to the stage and click the green flag icon, which can be found beside the big red circle. If the program does not encounter any errors while executing the blocks, the Sprite on the stage will say "Hello!". With this, our first program is a success! However, this is just the beginning, and we have a lot to learn about coding with Scratch!

Before we can close the current window and start a new project, we first need to name and save our program. To do this, we go to the toolbar, open the File menu, and select the 'Save project' option. Now we will be prompted to type in a name, follow the instructions, and then click the Save button to save your program onto the permanent storage of your Raspberry Pi.

SEQUENCING YOUR PROGRAMS

Sequencing is basically informing the computer to perform a series of actions in a defined sequence or order. Sequencing is an important concept to understand because if you want to create a program that performs multiple tasks in succession, then you will need to sequence those blocks of code which refer to such instructions. For example, our first program essentially only has one genuine instruction/task to perform, although it consists of two blocks. If we want to extend the number of tasks to be performed, we will need to know about sequencing.

Just as how a recipe has instructions laid out in chronological order, similarly, sequencing ensures that each instruction follows on from the last in a logical progression. This particular progression of instruction is also known as Linear Sequencing.

Let's learn more about this with the help of a demonstration. First, we will remove the 'Say Hello!' block. To do this, just drag the block and put it back to the block palette. We will only be left with the brown 'When clicked' block, the trigger block.

In this demonstration, we will use and sequence blocks such that our sprite will first move a certain distance, then perform a task and move back to its original position. Now, we will select the 'motion' category from the blocks palette. Among these blue blocks, we will find the 'move 10 steps' block, which we need, drag it and place it under the trigger block in the scripts area. To create a sequence, we still require more instructions (blocks). We will now select a sound block, move to a block palette, and choose the sound palette category. Over here, select the pink block 'play sound meow until done' and drop it under the blue block by dragging it to the scripts area. Still, not enough, let's go to the 'Motion' category again and select the 'move 10 steps' block but this time, click on the number specified in the block and change it to **-10** and add it below the pink block in the scripts area.

Now that we have imported a series of instructions and sequenced them, all that's left to do is run the program and see how it works. Click the green flag above the stage to run the program. We see that our sprite moves 10 units to the right, and after completing the first instruction, it stops and makes a meow sound (only heard if you have speakers or headphones connected to the Raspberry Pi), and then, it starts moving back to its original position. We have successfully created a sequence of multiple instructions which are executed by the Scratch in a top to bottom order.

Scratch performs these multiple tasks one at a time, while it may seem that the execution of these blocks of code should be slow, that's not the case. In fact, the computer would perform these actions so quickly that you will not even notice them. To better understand this, let's tweak the above program, which we have just created. Delete the 'play sound meow until done' and replace it with 'play meow sound' by placing it in the same position where the previous purple block was. Now simply run the program again, and you'll see that the sprite remains in its original position and also makes the meow sound. In reality, the sprite is moving, but the forward and backward motion is so fast that the sprite seems to be standing still, this is because the Raspberry Pi has the capability of performing tasks at an incredible speed such that it is ready to execute the next block before the first block is even finished. However, if you want the sprite to wait before moving back to its original position, you can do so by using the 'wait for 1 secs' golden blocks found in the 'Control' category of the blocks palette. Add this golden block after the purple sound block and click the green flag to run the program again. This time, instead of standing still, the sprite will move forward, make the sound, then wait an exact 1 second before moving back to its original position.

WORKING THROUGH LOOPS AND LOOPING

A sequence of blocks in Scratch is executed, and then the system goes idle, waiting for further instructions. For example, take the above program we have just designed. The cat moves ten units, meows, waits for one second, then moves back and stays there. The execution of the block sequence has been completed, and the system is waiting for the input of additional blocks in the script area until then it will stay idle. Any sequence of blocks you add in the scripts area will run only one time, then stop.

This is where loops come in. These are special blocks that put the entire sequence of blocks, in which they are added, on a self-repeating cycle (a loop). You can further specify the conditions and cycles of the loop, but that is an advanced concept. All we need to know is that we can make our block sequence repeat its execution for an indefinite number of times.

To use the loop block, simply go over to the block palette, and in the 'Control' category, select the 'forever' block. Drag it to the scripts area and drop it just above the sequence of blocks you want to loop. For demonstrative purposes, we will use the 'forever' block in the program we designed earlier. Place it just below the trigger block. You'll notice that the golden block automatically wraps around the rest of the block sequence in a C shape.

To test out the looping function of the block, click the green flag above the stage area to run these blocks in the scripts area. We can now see that the sprite in the stage continuously moves back and forth while meowing in between, instead of performing the same series of actions only once and then stopping. We have no successfully looped our program!

The loop we just used is one type out of many. This specific loop is known as an infinite loop because the sequence in which it is implemented, runs for an indefinite amount of times, or in other words, forever. Let's use another type of loop block this time. First, delete the current loop block. Move over to the block palette, in the 'Control' Category select the '**repeat 10**' block and drag-drop it under the trigger block as we did with the previous loop block. The sequence of blocks should look something like this:

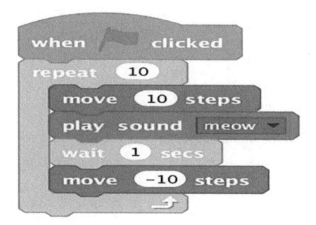

Now, run the program by clicking the green flag above the stage area. We can see that the sprite in the stage keeps repeating the same action as we observed in the 'forever' loop, but this time, the sprite will stop after performing the set of tasks exactly ten times. We can also categorize such specific loops a definite loops because the number of repetitions is defined, after which the looping sequence will exit. Loops are most commonly found in games and sensing programs, and the types of loops used are both indefinite and definite loops.

USING VARIABLES AND CONDITIONALS IN SCRATCH PROGRAMMING

A variable is an entity in a code whose value changes over time under the control of the program. Furthermore, variables and conditionals are closely related in terms of functionality and usage. Variables are very practical and useful when programming because you can manipulate them directly from your program after defining certain conditions and situations.

A variable associates itself with the following properties;

- The name that it is given

- The value it stores

The name is important because it will identify the variable, and you can only address or refer to the variable after specifying this name.

The value that can be stored by a variable is not limited to an integer. In fact, a variable is capable of storing numbers, texts, true or false values (Boolean expressions), or even empty values (null values).

These properties make variables a powerful and efficient tool. For example, think of all the things that have to be recorded and cross-checked in a game; you have the health point of a character, the speed of a moving object, the level which is currently being played, and the current score. These different types of information cannot be bundled together because they are innately unique in their respective types, and it is not possible to detail every small change in the values of these elements. This is where variables come in handy. Not only can you define each of these elements in a variable, but the change in each value is controlled directly by the program instead of the programmer. This is why variables are very important in programming as you can make your code more practical, efficient, and easy to write.

HOW TO USE VARIABLES AND CONDITIONALS

Before we go ahead and learn about how to use variables and conditionals, we first need to save the project we have been working on and open a new one. To do this, simply click the file drop-down list in the top taskbar and save the program by clicking the 'Save Project.' Now start a new project, go to the blocks palette, and over there, you'll see in the last row that there's a category 'Data.' Select this category and click the 'Make a Variable' button.

You're now halfway through making a Variable for your program. Before the Variable can be used in programming, you need to name it, for demonstrative purposes, we'll name our variable as 'loops,' click the OK button and now we will proceed to sequence blocks as we discussed previously.

We now need to go back to the blocks palette and add blocks to the scripts area. However, this time, we will use a slightly different approach in the blocks that we will choose for our program. First off, go to the 'Control' category and select the 'set loops to 0' block and drag it to the scripts area. This block basically instructs the computer to set the value of our loops variable to 0. Now we need an action block for our sprite, go to blocks palette, and under the 'Action' category, drag the 'say Hello! for 2 sec' block just beneath the orange block in the scripts area.

Here comes the part where we will utilize the variable in our program to influence sprite's action. As we have used the sound block 'say Hello! for 2 sec', we have the choice to change the phrase which the sprite will repeat. Instead of writing the desired message or phrase in the purple block by ourselves, we can use the variable to do the job for us. For this, go to blocks palette and under the 'Data' category and look for a **rounded 'loops' block,** which is commonly at the top of the list accompanied by a tick box next to it. Instead of how we normally place loop blocks, drag this rounded orange block and place it over the word 'Hello!' in the purple block placed in the scripts area. We have now created a new combined block.

This rounded orange block is also known as a reporter block, and it basically imports the value of the variable it refers to onto the block in which it is incorporated. Before testing it out, we need a trigger block to complete the program. Just drag and add the 'when clicked' brown block from the 'Events' category and place it above the orange block. Now we're ready to run this program. Go to the stage area and click the green flag icon, the program executes successfully, and we can see the sprite in the stage area displays a message '**0**'. This message is the value of the variable stored in the orange block to which we referred to by using the reporter block to fetch the referral value and use it as the message in the sound block. In fact, we can also say that this message is basically the value that we gave to the variable 'loops' in the beginning.

As discussed before, the value of a variable can be changed directly from the program itself as the code progresses. Since we have established the method of how to use a variable, let's proceed to change the value of a variable. It's quite simple, actually. Go to the blocks palette and drag the orange block 'change loops by 1', which you can find under the 'Control' category, directly beneath the purple block in the scripts area. Along with this, drag and drop a looping block as well. You can see that we have used a 'repeat 10' block placed directly beneath the variable 'set loops to 0'.

The purpose of the golden loop block is that it effectively demonstrates the changing of the 'loops' variable because we have used 'change loops by 1'. So every time the sequence of blocks is repeated, the variable changes by 1. Once it completes its first cycle, the value of the variable will have become 1, on the second cycle, the value would be 2, on the third cycle, the value would be three and so on until the loop is finished.

To see it for yourself, click the green flag, and you'll see the sprite is counting from 0 to 9 instead of just displaying 0. Every time the loop runs, a value of '1' is added to the variable, and hence, the program is actually modifying the variable by itself.

EXTENDING THE USE OF A VARIABLE

The functionality and usefulness of variables do not stop at the modification of their values. Let's use the combination of variables and loops in a slightly different way. To demonstrate this, we will first remove the 'repeat 10' loop block from the sequence and replace it with a 'repeat until' block (double-check that the 'repeat until' block is connected to all the other blocks in the sequence). The new looping block we have just added also has a diamond-shaped empty space. This empty space is a slot for adding operators. Such a block is incomplete without an operator, so to add operators, we will go to the blocks palette and under the 'Operators' category, select the diamond-shaped comparative operator block, drag and drop it onto the empty space in the 'repeat until' block.

The function of this operator block is just as its name suggests; it directly compares two values and the type of values it can compare also include variables, which is why we are using such an operator in this demonstration. So far, the operator block is empty, and we need to input the values we want to compare. To do this, we will once again select the rounded orange 'loops' block, also known as reporter block, and drag-drop it into the left-hand side of the comparison equation in the operator block. We will enter the second value as 10 (although this value can be anything). We are now comparing the value of a variable to an integer.

Let's see what happens when we run the program now. Upon clicking the green flag button, we come to see that the sprite simply counts to 9 and stops, just as it did with the 'repeat until 10' loop block. But there's a very significant difference in how the code is actually functioning. Rather than repeating the execution of the block sequence for a defined number of times, the program actually compares the value of the variable directly to the other value in the comparative equation. This means that the program repeats itself until the 'loops' variable's value finally becomes '10'.

Apart from the '=' comparative operator, if you go over to the block palette and select the 'Operators' category, you'll find two other diamond shaped operators as well with different operators, namely;

- The lesser than comparative operator '<' (directly compares any two values and is triggered when the left-hand side value is found to be smaller than the right-hand side value)

- The greater than comparative operator '>' (directly compares any two values and is triggered when the left-hand side value is found to be greater than the right-hand side value)

USING CONDITIONALS ALONGSIDE VARIABLES

Conditionals are basically **"IF-THEN," "IF-ELSE,"** and **"IF-THEN-ELSE"** statements. The function of these statements is similar to what they emphasize. Before textually explaining how these statements work, let's use the above demonstration to understand how are they used in a sequence of blocks and how they affect the working of the said sequence of blocks.

To use the conditional blocks, go over to the 'Control' category in the blocks palette, and look for the 'if-then' block. Drag this block into the scripts area, placing it under combined 'say loops for 2 secs' block. Due to the function of this block, we can observe that as soon as we place it beneath the purple combined block, it immediately surrounds the orange 'change loops by 1' block. But we don't want it to do that, so we will manually change its position by dragging the orange block and placing it beneath the 'if-then' block. We need to fill the conditional statement. To do this, move to the blocks palette and add a 'say Hello! for 2 secs' block from the sounds category inside the 'if-then' block. Now to add the operator. Just as we did with the 'repeat until' block, add a diamond-shaped ">" operator block from the 'Operators' category and place it into the empty space in the 'if-then' block.

Now onto explain the purpose of the conditional block, we just added into the above sequence. In simple terms, the 'if-then' conditional block controls the execution of blocks, which it envelops. In the above demonstration, we can see that the conditional block is enveloping 'say Hello! for 2 secs' block, this sequence will only be run by the program if the condition set by the 'if-then' block is fulfilled. If the condition is not fulfilled, the computer will skip over the conditional block during code execution.

We will now add a condition statement into the 'if-then' block. Add the same reporter block we used previously, the rounded 'loops' block from the 'Data' category of the blocks palette, in the left-hand side of the comparative statement, and on the right-hand side, we will enter a number, for example, let's use 5. We can also edit the message in the purple block, let's change the message from "Hello!" to "That's high!".

Our block sequence is now complete and ready for testing. Click the green flag in the stage area to run the program. Initially, we will see that the program is running in the same way as before, the sprite counting in an ascending order starting from 0. However, things change when the sprite reaches number 5. According to the condition we have outlined in the conditional block, if the variable's value exceeds 5, then block enveloped by the 'if-then' block will be executed by the program. This is proved by the cat displaying the message "That's high!" according to the 'say That's high! for 2 secs' block.

These are the basics of working with variables and conditionals.

EXPLANATORY EXAMPLE: REACTION TIMER ASTRONAUT

There are multiple free source projects available online to help you challenge your programming skills with the Raspberry Pi by providing you with fun and creative projects to create in Scratch. We will go through such projects as educational examples.

The first project which we will take up is the astronaut reaction timer application. But before we begin, you should know about a few things, one that this project depends on two pictures for, a space background and an astronaut character (sprite). Both of these are not included in the resources of Scratch, which is why we need to download it from the internet. Connect your Raspberry Pi to the internet and open the chromium-browser. Type in the following URL into the address bar of chromium, **rpf.io/astronaut-backdrop**, once you've done that, simply hit enter, and you'll be taken to a page where you'll be greeted by a picture of the space filled with tiny shiny stars and a small portion of the earth. Save this picture by right-clicking on it and selecting 'Save image as' and select the destination in which you want to save the file; we will be using the downloads folder in this case. After saving this image, clear the URL in the address bar with the backspace and enter the following URL, **rpf.io/astronaut-sprite,** and hit Enter. This time, you will be greeted by an astronaut performing some weird acrobatics, we will use this image as the sprite for our project. Save this image by repeating the process, and after you're done, close the chromium web browser and open the Scratch 2 tab once again.

Now that we have the required sprite and background image, we will first replace the sprite currently on the stage with the astronaut. To do this, simply right click the character on the stage and select the delete option from the list of options. This will remove the sprite from the stage. Now the stage is set for setting up the space background and astronaut sprite. Navigate to the bottom left of the Scratch 2 window, and there you'll find the stage controls through which you can import the background and sprite directly to the stage. There will be an upload backdrop icon, click that, and a small window will pop up, navigate to the folder where you downloaded the image and double click it, after the image uploads onto the Scratch 2 application, the once plain white background will now turn into a stellar image of space. You can also see the same image on the scripts area; this is so that you can draw on the image and edit it according to your liking before finalizing it for the stage to use, as you edit it, you can see how it will look on the stage side by side. To return the scripts area back to its original form, click on the tab marked 'scripts,' and the image will go away.

Now on to uploading our newly saved sprite. The process is similar, just select the upload sprite icon in the stage controls (this icon can be found right next to the 'new sprite'). When the small window pop-ups, navigate to the folder where you saved the sprite image and double click it. The window will automatically close, and on the stage, you'll see the sprite with its happy smile looking at you. Although the sprite has been successfully added, the position of the sprite doesn't need always to be correct. In case the position is a little bit off, you can adjust it by holding it with your mouse's left-click and dragging it where you want it to be. In our case, we want the sprite to be in the lower-middle position.

Now that we have successfully added our new background and sprite, we are set for proceeding with the project by moving on to the next step, and that is creating the program.

The main function of our program is to be a reaction timer. So the first thing we need to do is to define a variable. In this case, we'll create a variable with the name 'time' so it's easy to understand.

Also, keep in mind that before clicking OK, check the 'For all sprites' box below the name field. Now in the sprites pane, select the sprite on which the blocks of code will take action. It's important to specify sprites in cases where you are working with multiple characters on a stage, but luckily in our case, there's only one sprite to work with. From here on out, we'll proceed without explaining every little detail as we have discussed them extensively in the previous sections of the chapter. Follow the steps accordingly;

1. Add a trigger block 'when clicked' into the scripts area

2. From the 'Looks' category, add the 'say Hello! for 2 secs' block and change the default greeting from "Hello!" to "Hello! British ESA Astronaut Tim Peake here. Are you ready?"

3. We will now add four more blocks chronologically in the following sequence, first the 'wait 1-sec' block which can be found in the 'Control' category followed by a 'say Hello!' purple block (rewrite the default message of this block from 'say Hello!' to 'Hit Space!'). After adding the purple block, go to the 'Sensing' category in the blocks palette and look for the 'reset timer' block and add it (the 'reset timer' block basically controls a special pre-built variable in the Scratch program. This variable is used for timing things; in our project, it will be involved in timing how quickly the user will react in the game). Finally, we need to add a combined block, which will prompt the user to press a key and simultaneously pause the game without

freezing the timer until the specific key is pressed. To do this, we will add a golden 'wait until' block and drag a 'keyspace pressed?' (to determine whether the specified key has been pressed or not) sensing block into the empty space.

4. We now need to display the message detailing how long it took for the user to react and press the Space key. To do this, we need a block made by concatenation (taking two different values and joining them together). Add a purple 'say Hello!' block and drag-drop a new green 'Join' operator block onto the word 'Hello!' in the purple block. This will make a new combined block. There is an empty space in the new combined block; we will fill it with the phrase "Your reaction time was." That's not enough; we still need to add in the reaction time recorded by the 'reset timer' block. Bring in another 'Join' operator block and drop it into the same combined block; this will make another Join space. Add the blue rounded 'timer' reporting block found in the 'Sensing' category into the newly added 'Join' block. Don't forget to add the phrase "seconds." Into the last box so that the sentence displayed is complete. Also, notice how we have intentionally left an empty space at the end of the phrase "Your reaction time was," this is done to ensure that there is an empty space between the two joined values.

5. To wrap things up, we will add a small timer window onto the stage. To do this, go to the 'Data' category and select the 'set time to 0' variable block and attach it to the end of the

sequence of your blocks. Replace the 0 with the reporting block 'timer,' and you're now good to go. Startup the program and hit the space button as soon as you see the message.

EXPLANATORY EXAMPLE: SWIMMING IN SYNC

The next project we will be focusing on is one which emphasizes on two-button control (mostly the left and right arrow) instead of one button controls.

Let's start building the project! If you are already using the Scratch 2 application, save the current project, and open a new one. Let's name this new project, "Swimming in Sync." The theme this time is swimming, so a cat will work just fine cause our sprite knows how to swim (hopefully).

CHANGING THE BACKGROUND

Let's change the background a bit to make it suit the theme of the project. Instead of using an image for the stage background, we'll just change the color to an ocean blue. To do this, go to the stage controls and navigate to the backdrops tab. Over here, you'll see that there is a color palette at the bottom; from that palette, choose the ocean-blue color and fill the color with the bucket icon. It's kind of like how you'd edit the background in Microsoft Paint.

CHANGING THE SPRITE

Instead of using the default cat sprite, we'll use a slightly different version of it. This time, however, we will not need to go over to an external website and download a sprite; instead, we will select a sprite from Scratch's sprite library. Before adding a sprite, delete the current one by right-clicking and selecting delete. Afterward, If you look below, you'll notice 'New sprite' accompanied by four icons. Select the first one. This will take you directly to the sprite library. In the library, navigate to the animals' category and see if there's any sprite that suits the theme. For now, we will choose 'Cat1 Flying' sprite as it somewhat gives the image that it's swimming. Add the new sprite by clicking ok.

After choosing a sprite from the library, we will now proceed to add code blocks and sequencing them.

ADDING CODE BLOCKS

For starters, go over to the 'Events' category in the blocks palette and look for the 'when space key pressed' blocks. We need two of these event blocks, so drag this block two times into the scripts area. This block code basically triggers an event whenever the key specified on it is pressed. The trigger key can be changed, as well.

After adding the two trigger blocks, notice that each of the brown blocks have a small arrow beside the word 'space' click on it and you'll be presented a list of possible keys that can be bound to the block. In that list, select 'left arrow' for the first block and 'right arrow' for the second block.

After specifying the key, go to the 'Motions' category in the blocks palette and add a 'turn left 15 degrees' block under the 'when left

71

arrow key pressed' block and similarly, add 'turn right 15 degrees' block under the 'when right arrow key pressed' block.

Before moving forward, test it out by simply pressing the left or right arrow keys on the keyboard. You'll be able to see that the sprite turns in a direction matching the arrow key you press. The reason why we do not need to use the green flag to run the program is that the event trigger block we are using this time is different, i.e., the trigger is a keypress. This means that the event trigger blocks are active the entire time the program is running.

Now that we have defined the action of the left and right arrow keys let's do the same for the up and down arrow keys. Bring in two 'when space key pressed' blocks, change the trigger key from 'space' key to 'up' and 'down' arrow key, respectively. For the motion blocks this time, instead of using the ones that turn the sprites in a specific direction, we will use the 'move 10 steps' block to associate it with the Up arrow key and the 'move -10 steps' block to associate it with the 'Down' arrow key.

CHANGING THE APPEARANCE OF THE SPRITE

We can change the appearance of the sprite to make the motion seem much more realistic to the user. These changes to the appearance can be made by using **Costumes**. To add a costume to our sprite, all we need to do is select the sprite from the sprites pane and simply click the costume tab, which can be found above the blocks palette. Delete the current appearance 'cat1 flying a' and select the 'cat1 flying b' costume. We will use this specific costume for whenever we press the right arrow key, and to make things easier, let's rename this costume to from 'cat1 flying b' to 'right.'

We also want to use the same costume facing in the opposite direction whenever we press our left arrow key. Instead of deleting and adding it again, just right-click the costume and select the duplicate option. In this new copy of the costume, flip the costume by clicking on the flip left-right icon and rename it to 'left.'

CODING THE CHANGING COSTUMES INTO THE SCRIPTS AREA

To associate a specific costume to a trigger event block, or in simple terms, when a key is pressed in our program, simply add the 'switch costume to' block (from the 'Looks' category in the blocks palette) directly underneath each of the brown event trigger blocks such that It comes between the motion block and the event blocks. Since we only have two costumes, we will only add it to the left and right arrow key event blocks.

ADDING MORE SPRITES AND SYNCHRONIZING THEIR MOTION

We have no reached the final stage of our project. As its common knowledge that synchronized swimming cannot be done with a single swimmer alone. You need more than one swimmers, so we will be adding more sprites to the stage and adjusting their position and motion, respectively.

Add a separate 'when clicked' event trigger block as the last block in the sequence so far and underneath this brown trigger block, throw in a 'go-to x: 0 y: 0' block from the 'Motions' category in the blocks palette. From the category of the same motion, add the 'point in direction 90' block to define the way that the cat will face as soon as the event is triggered. For instance, if you click the green flag right now, you'll see that the cat's position would be the middle of the stage, pointing to the right direction, all according to the coordinates and position we defined in the block sequence.

Now we'll proceed to add more swimmers. Adding more swimmers is a relatively easy job, simply go over to the 'Control' category and drag in a 'repeat 10' block. But we don't need ten swimmers; seven will suffice. As we already have one swimmer ready to go, change the value of the 'repeat 10' block to 'repeat 6' and pair it up with 'create a clone of myself block.' With this combination of blocks, the swimmers will clone themselves without the need of having to duplicate and insert them manually. But there's one issue, as the sprites will spawn, all of them are going to be swimming in the same direction by default, to change this, simply add a 'turn right 60-degree' motion block between the 'create a clone' and 'repeat 6' block. Each time the code loops, the spawned swimmer's direction will be 60 degrees to the right than the one spawned before it.

This still doesn't give off the Olympic synchronized swimmer feel. Let's add a bit of music to spice things up. To add music, navigate to the sounds tab, located just above the blocks palette, and select the option 'choose a new sound from sound library' (which is accompanied by a small speaker icon). In the sound library, there are a bunch of categories. Find the 'Music Loops' category and click it, this will open up a side window displaying a lot of music sounds. Browse through these multiple sound files until you come across something that piques your interest. For this project, let's select the 'dance around' music file. Choose the music file by selecting it and clicking the OK button.

Now that we've selected the right music for our synchronized swimmers to jam to, we need to loop it so that it keeps on playing and does not stop. To do this, we will use the indefinite 'forever' loop. But before that, add the 'when clicked' event trigger block and pair it with the 'forever' loop block and the 'play sound dance around until done' block (from the sound category).

We can now finally proceed to simulate an entire dancing routine. To do this, add a new event trigger followed by;

- 'When space key pressed' event block

- 'Switch costume to right' block

- 'Repeat 36' block (change the value from the default 10)

- 'Turn right 10 degrees' block

- 'Move 10 steps' block

The entire block sequence so far should look like this:

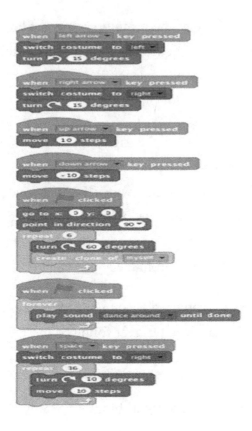

We have now finished the project. To try out the new synchronized swimming routine, press the SPACE key. Don't forget to save the program while you're having fun with it!

Chapter 5

Working With Python

In contrast to the visual programming with Scratch, python moves towards a more traditional approach towards computer programming. Python uses a text-based code that instructs the computer to carry out certain tasks. Following up on the fundamentals we learned in Scratch with the Python will greatly complement our learning of computer programming.

Fundamentally, python requires precise writing of code, but it also offers a friendly user interface where you are guided along the way of writing codes by the application itself (marking mistakes in code and offering useful suggestions).

The Raspberry Pi already has a Python Integrated Development Environment by the name of Thonny Python IDE. Open this up by going to the Raspberry Pi menu, and under the programming category, look for this application.

INTRODUCTION TO THE PYTHON EDITOR AND CONTROL INTERFACE

Thonny is a special application package. The reason why it is called an 'Integrated Development Environment' is because of its function. As the name suggests, it firstly integrates (or gathers) all of the tools that a user would require to write code into this application. Given access to all the necessary tools, the user can now develop software onto a single environment (interface). On a basic level, it performs three different and distinct functions so that we can write code in the Python programming language.

This specific integrated development environment for python has two modes. A Normal mode and a Simple mode. The simple mode makes things even easier for beginners, and in this guide, we will be referring to the Simple model of this application. Using the **Simple Mode** of the Thonny Python IDE, let's label and explain the components of the application.

1. This is the toolbar that you'll see while in the application's Simple Mode. Beneath each friendly icon on the toolbar, you'll see that they are labeled with the purpose for which they are used.

2. This is the application's script area. The purpose of this area is exactly similar to the Scratch application. We write down codes in this area, the numbering on the left side of this area indicates the line number. As you keep writing codes, it's automatically indexed. In the scenario where your code encounters an error, you will know which line of code the error is referring to and because every line is indexed, you can quickly navigate to the faulty line of code and fix it. This simple indexing can be pretty useful and time-saving.

3. This is the Python Shell. This area provides information about the code which is currently being run by the application and also, you can input individual lines of code and execute them by simply pressing the ENTER button.

4. This is specifically the variables area. This area shows you information (name and value) of all the variables that you created for a specific program.

PROGRAMMING WITH PYTHON: MAKING A PROGRAM

After you start up python, the first thing you will notice is that, unlike Scratch, there are no colorful blocks or sprites. This is because Python is more of a traditional programming language that relies on code being manually written down (without any typos or errors, of course!).

However, this does not make Python difficult or hard to handle. In fact, with a little practice, Python can be as easy to use as Scratch. For instance, let's demonstrate how easy it is to create a simple program on python.

Open up python from the Raspberry Pi menu and wait for Thonny Python IDE to load up (Thonny will start-up in the Simple Mode by default). Go over to the Python shell area (described in the previous section) and type in

Print("Good Morning!"**)**

After typing in the following instruction, all you need to do is press the **ENTER** key, and you'll see the message "Good Morning" displayed below the instruction. We have just created our first program. It was as simple as that!

Before we move on, let's explain what does the above line of code actually represents. Well, the code has basically three elements; The function statement, in this case, **Print**, the parenthesis, and the message inside the quotation marks. The **Print** function statement basically tells the computer to display a message inside the parenthesis quotation marks. Throughout this chapter, we will learn a variety of different function statements that do interesting stuff.

On to the Python Shell Area and the difference between the shell area and the scripts area. Basically, the Python Shell Area is somewhat of a direct line to the Python Interpreter. Anything you type into the Shell Area will be immediately interpreted and responded, kind of like how face to face conversations work. Just as how we hold a conversation by saying something and waiting for the other person to respond and vice versa, the Shell area works similarly. We do not write entire blocks of code into this area. Instead, we just input individual lines of code to test them out or to see their results. The scripts area is for inputting the entire code, which your program will contain as the end result. Moreover, you cannot input multiple lines of code into the Shell area because it's not made for that. As soon as you hit **ENTER**, the code will execute. On the other hand, when you press **ENTER** after writing a line of code, instead of executing the lines of code, you just get a new blank line to write more code. To execute the codes in the scripts area, you need to do so by clicking the 'Run' icon in the toolbar (When you click the Run button, Thonny will prompt you to save your current program first, just type in a name for your program and click save). Notice that when you run a saved program from the scripts area, the message in the shell area is a bit different this time

>>> **%Run 'Name you used to save the program.py.'**
Good Morning!

You can also write the same line of code in the scripts area as well, but this time, we'll use a different and more popular phrase "Hello, World!" and while saving it, we will give it the name **Hello, World!**

(Here's the message you'll see in the shell area)

>>> **%Run 'Hello World.py'**

Hello, World!

The First line basically instructs the Interpreter to execute the program, which has just been saved, and the second line is the end result or the output of running that program, in our case, displaying a message. We have successfully written our first program on Python and ran it in both interactive and script modes.

USING LOOPS AND CODE INDENTATION

We have learned the purpose of loops in programming, but code indentation is a new concept when coming from Scratch to Python programming.

Indentation is basically python's way of controlling the sequence in which the lines of code are executed. In Scratch programming, we would use the colorful blocks and place them above each other in the sequence, which we wanted, but in Python, we need to use indentation to tell the computer that this is the sequence in which the lines of code are to be run.

Open a new project by clicking on the 'New' icon in the toolbar. This will open a separate new window for you to work on. In the scripts area, type in the following lines of code;

print("Loop starting!")

for i in range (10):

In the above lines of code, the first line works exactly in the same way as demonstrated in the **Print(**"Good Morning"**)** example. However, the second line is rather interesting. This line actually initiates a definite loop sequence, with the defined limit being set by the **range** followed by the desired integer. The **i** is the loop counter which will count the number of times the program loops, in this case, it will count upwards till nine because the stop instruction is the number 10, as soon as the 9th loop is completed, the loop will exit. Also, look at the colon "**:**" at the end of the line. This tells the computer that the following lines of code are actually a part of the loop.

Moreover, in Scratch, we saw that the instruction which is to be added into the loop function could be placed on the loop block directly. But in Python, we indent the instruction code by using a colon (":"). An indentation is characterized by four blank spaces left at the beginning of the new line; the IDE application does this automatically as soon as you press **ENTER** after an indentation.

```
print("Loop starting!")
for i in range (10):
    print("Loop number", i)
```

This indentation is what allows python to differentiate between instructions that are not included in the loop and instructions, which are to be included in the loop (this indented code is known as being nested).

All the lines following this indentation will automatically contain four blank spaces because Thonny assumes that the following lines of code will also be the part of the loop. This will keep happening until you have written all the instructions which are part of the loop. To close the indentation, simply make a new indented blank line and press **BACKSPACE**, this will return the line back to normal. Now, close the indentation as described and write the following line of code

> **print("Loop finished!")**

> The sequence of the lines of code should be something like this;

> **print("Loop starting!")**

> **for i in range (10):**

>> **print("Loop number", i)**

> **print("Loop finished!")**

In this program, the first line and last line is outside of the loop because they are not indented. The second line is where the loop starts and contains the indentation, whereas the third line is part of the loop.

Let's save this program as "indentation" and run the program. In the shell area, we will see the following output;

> Loop starting!

> Loop number 0

> Loop number 1

> Loop number 2

> Loop number 3

> Loop number 4

Loop number 5

Loop number 6

Loop number 7

Loop number 8

Loop number 9

Loop finished!

The reason why Python counts from zero instead of one is that Python is designed as a zero-indexed language. This means that it considers 0 as the beginning integer rather than 1. You can change this behavior by specifying the range instruction to be a range (1, 11) instead of range(10). With this, the loop will start counting from 1 to 10. You can do this for any number you want.

Just as how we used definite and indefinite loops in Scratch, the same can be done in Python. To use indefinite loops (loops that run forever), all you need to do is edit the 2nd line of code in the above program.

```
print("Loop starting!")
While True:
    print("Loop running!")
print("Loop finished!")
```

You have now created an indefinite loop. This is because the end condition of the loop has not been specified as each time the message "loop running!" is printed, the program directs the code execution back to the start, and the whole process is repeated until the program itself is terminated. Save the program and run it to see the output in the shell area.

To terminate the program, simply click the red 'Stop' icon. The program will terminate without ever being able to reach the last line of the code.

USING CONDITIONALS AND VARIABLES

In Scratch programming, we mostly used variables and conditionals to control loops and how they worked. But there's more to variables than just controlling loops. Adding variables in python is different than adding variables in Scratch.

Open up a new project by clicking the 'New' icon and in the scripts area, input the following line of code

userName = input ("What is your name? ")

Save the program and run it. The output of this program is that it displays a message asking for your name. After the end of the message, left-click the empty space, write a name, and hit ENTER. Nothing will happen in the program, but if you shift your focus to the right towards the variables window, you'll see that a variable 'userName' assigned with the value you just entered has been created.

Now that we have added a variable, let us proceed to the fun part, making the program do something useful with the inputted name.

To demonstrate how to use variables in python, we will pair the 'userName' variable with a conditional statement. In this demonstration, the program will ask us for our name, and based on our answer, it will give us a specific response.

if userName == "Clark Kent":

　　print("You are Superman!")

else:

　　print("You are not Superman!")

Now run the program after saving it and notice the output. In the first scenario, when the program asks us for our name, it compares it with the variable's value "Calrk Kent" to see if it matches. If our name matches the one in the variable, then the condition is said to be True; if it does not match, then the condition is said to be False. Depending on the result being True or False, the conditional statement instructs the program to execute one of the following lines of code.

Also, notice that instead of one equality "=" symbol, we used a double equality symbol "==." This is because a single equality symbol actually assigns a value to a variable, or in simpler terms, make this value equal to this variable. While the double equality symbol makes a direct comparison. One is an assigning operator, while the other is a comparative operator.

Also, a text in quotation marks is referred to as a **String**. A number with or without quotation marks is referred to as an **Integer**. When you are combining two different types of information, for example, the text "How old are you?" with the reply **22**, you will have to convert the integer into a string before they can be joined. But that's an advanced concept and will be discussed in higher levels of this guide.

When working with numbers, you can also use the greater than '>' and lesser than '<' comparative operators. But to use the equal to operator, you'll have to use '==.' Similarly, equal to or greater than '=>' and equal to or less than '=<' can also be used.

We will now use some comparison operators in the loop example we used previously.

> **while userName != "Clark Kent":**
>
> > **print("You are not Superman – try again!")**
> >
> > **userName = input ("what is your name")**
>
> **print("You are Superman!)**

Upon running this program, you'll see that instead of quitting the program after telling you that you are not superman, it will keep inquiring your name until it is confirmed that you are indeed the superhero Superman. This is the basic framework of how you can program a simple password mechanism.

EXPLANATORY EXAMPLE: FLOWER SNOWFLAKES

In this example, we will play to understand how python really works by creating a graphical demonstration using this language.

Before proceeding, it is important to know that for this demonstration, we will be using a tool or an add-on code. This code is actually present in the library of the Python but not being used by the python itself. It is dormant. To use this tool, we need to import it into our project, remember that when you start a new project, you will have to import tools and functions again because they reset each time.

So for this explanatory example, we will be importing a tool known as 'turtle.' This tool stops or starts drawing a line as it moves. We will be using this function to create our graphical representation of flower snowflakes.

Open a new project in Thonny and type this code;

Import turtle

We have successfully imported the instructions present in the turtle tool but here's the catch, whenever we type out instruction from this tool, we first need to reference the name of the tool itself, and after a full stop, we then type out the instruction. Repeatedly doing this can make writing a code a really annoying job, so for the sake of convenience, we'll assign a variable to this tool so that we don't have to type out its full name before every instruction repeatedly. The variable we will be using is 'tim.'

tim = turtle. Turtle()

Let's test this variable out

tim.forward(100)

Save the program and run it. However, this time, you won't need to check the Python shell area for the output, but instead, a new window will pop up named 'Turtle Graphics' on which the result of your instruction will be displayed. A line of 100 units across will be drawn.

Close this window and switch back to the main Thonny application. Now we are going to type out a series of codes in the scripts area.

for i in range(2):

    tim.forward(100)

    tim.right(60)

    tim.forward(100)

    tim.right(120)

After running this program, we can see that a shape resembling that of a parallelogram has been drawn on the Turtle Graphics window. Now we are going to turn this shape into a snowflake;

```
Import turtle
tim = turtle.Turtle()
for i in range(10):
for i in range(2):
tim.forward(100)
im.right(60)
tim.forward(100)
tim.right(120)
tim.right(36)
```

This code has a loop. Once the turtle tool has finished drawing a parallelogram, it will turn 36 degrees to the right and start drawing another one. This process will repeat until you'll see that there are a total of ten parallelograms on the Turtle Graphics window. Now to add a little color to the plain white screen, use the following lines of code

Turtle.Screen().bgcolor("blue")

tim.color("cyan")

The above code turns the color of the background to blue and the snowflake to cyan.

Apart from choosing and specifying a color, you can write a code that will choose the colors randomly. But for this, you will need to import another tool from the library

Import random

After importing the "random" tool, change the above background from blue to grey, and create a variable named 'colors.'

colors = ["cyan," "purple," "white," "blue"]

Notice how we used square brackets instead of the usual round brackets. This is because we have used a different type of variable known as a "list variable," and the use of square brackets characterizes this type. Although the list contains four possible colors for the snowflake segments, Python still needs to be instructed to choose a different color every time the loop repeats. Just write the following code at the end, but make sure it's indented.

tim.color(random.choice(colors))

Run the program again, and you'll see that as each petal is being drawn, Python is choosing a different color for each one.

These petals look more like the sharp ninja shurikens instead of a flower or even a snowflake for that matter. So let's change things up a little bit. Follow the code written below;

```
import turtle
import random
tim =turtle.Turtle()
turtle.Screen().bgcolor(grey)
colors = ["cyan," "white," "purple," "blue"]
tim.penup()
tim.forward(90)
tim.left(45)
tim.pendown()
def branch():
        for i in range(3):
        for i in range(3):
                tim.forward(30)
                tim.backward(30)
                tim.right(45)
```

```
            tim.left(90)

            tim.backward(30)

            tim.left(45)

        tim.right(90)

        tim.forward(90)

    for i in range(8)

        branch()

        tim.left(45)

#       pat.color(random.choice(colors))
```

Notice how the last line has a "#" symbol. This is used for adding comments to your code. Python ignores comments, and you can use comments to add explanations to your code or any line of your code, so it will be easier to understand if you send it to someone or if you look back on it after a few months.

Run this program, and this time, you'll see an image that actually depicts a snowflake.

EXPLANATORY EXAMPLE: WEED OUT IRREGULARITIES

This example will take help from a project available at rpf.io/scary-spot

Basically, this is a game where the player is shown two similar-looking images, but one of the images has a few anomalies (differences). After having a preliminary look at the original image, the player is then shown a composite image where a few things are changed. The player is required to weed out all the irregularities in the image.

For this game, we require the following components;

An original image

A scary surprise image (according to the theme we have chosen for the game)

A sound file

To get these files, we need to access the internet and download them directly on to our Raspberry Pi. To do this, go to the Chromium browser and in the address bar, enter the following URL

Rpf.io/spot-pic

You'll be redirected to a website that is displaying a conjoined (two) spooky image of a witch concocting some sort of potion. Right-click and save this image to wherever you want it (preferably somewhere you can easily navigate to). Now we need to download a scary and surprising picture to startle the player. Go to the chromium web browser and clear the address bar if there's a URL in it already. Enter the following URL

rpf.io/scary-pic

Hit ENTER, and you'll be redirected to a website displaying a picture of a zombie. Quite startling if something like this suddenly pops up! Save this image to the same place you saved the previous image. Now all that's left is to get a sound file that fits the theme. A scream would add really much to the production value so once again, open the chromium web browser, clear the address bar and type in the following URL

rpf.io/scream

Hit ENTER. This time instead of being taken to a website, the browser will automatically start to download a .wav format audio file. This is our scream sound file, which we will use to startle the player paired with the scary zombie image. However, we need to move the sound file to another directory before we can use this in our Python project. Open the file manager from the Raspberry Pi menu and go the 'Downloads' directory. Locate the scream.wav file in this directory, and right-click copy it. Go to the 'Pi' folder from the list to your left side inside the file manager and paste it there. Job's done, you can now close the file manager and Chromium web browser. Time to open up Thonny and start programming!

In this project, we'll be using the **pygame library**. So the first thing is to import this library into the project.

import pygame

This library alone is not enough to do the job; we'll need a bunch of other libraries as well as importing sub-libraries from the pygame. When importing sub-libraries, you need to use the 'from' in addition to the 'import' function.

Do this by writing the following lines of code;

from pygame.locals import *

from time import sleep

from random import randrange

The main difference between the from and import function is that 'form' is used to import only a portion of a library while the 'import' function imports the entire library.

Next up is initializing the pygame library; this is necessary to let the computer know that we are now set up to use this library's functionalities. To set up or initialize the pygame library, use;

pygame.init()

We also need to give python the details of our display's resolution, i.e., the width and height of the screen we are using as the display connected to the Raspberry Pi system. We can pass on the details of our current resolution to Python by using the following lines of code;

width = pygame.display.   Info().current_w

height = pygame.display.Info().current_h

There's only one thing left in setting up Pygame, and that is to create a screen, which is actually a window on which the game will display itself. To create the game's screen, use the following code;

screen = pygame.display.set_mode((width, height))

pygame.quit()

The empty space between the above two lines of code is not intentional; in fact, it is in this space that we will write the code for programming the behavior of our game. Before going further, let's check how does the program work so far, save the project and run the program. You'll see that a separate window is created, which only displays a background and disappears as soon as it appears because Python reaches the quit instruction right after displaying the screen. Alongside, numerous variables are also created as we ran this program, but this does not concern us for the time being, so ignore these variables.

We will now upload the image which will be displayed on the screen for the user to see and weed out the irregularities. In the empty space between the last two lines of code, enter the following code;

contrast = pygame.image.load('spot_the_diff.png')

After uploading this image to python, we need to match the resolution of the image with the resolution of the screen.

difference = pygame.transform.scale(difference (width, height))

screen.blit(difference, (0, 0))

pygame.display.update()

The last two lines of code actually tell the Python to fetch the images stored in the memory and display it on the screen so that the user can see it. The process of fetching data from the Random

Access Memory of the system and displaying it on the Screen is known as bit block transfer.

You can also make the image stay on screen for longer amounts of time by using the 'sleep' command.

sleep(3)

Now to add the spooky surprise to our game. Add the following lines of code;

pygame.display.update()

zombie = pygame.image.load('scary_face.png')

zombie = pygame.transform.scale (zombie, (width, height))

sleep(randrange(5, 15))   #This delays the program for a random amount of time between 5 and 15 seconds

screen.blit(zombie, (0, 0))

pygame.display.update()

We have now uploaded the scary image onto Python's memory and programmed it to be displayed on the screen for a random amount of time. All that's left is to add the sound file to our game. To do this, add the following lines of code;

scream = pygame.mixer.Sound('scream.wav')

#Add this line below the sleep command so the sound file plays before the image is displayed

scream.play()

#To tell the pygame to stop playing the sound file, add the following line of code;

scream.stop()

The finished code should be like this;

import pygame

from pygame.locals import *

from time import sleep

from random import randrange

pygame.init()

width = pygame.display.Info().current_w

height = pygame.display.Info().current_h

screen = pygame.display.set_mode((width, height))

difference = pygame.image.load('spot_the_diff.png')

difference = pygame.transform.scale(difference, (width, height))

screen.blit(difference, (0, 0))

```
pygame.display.update()

zombie = pygame.image.load('scary_face.png')

zombie = pygame.transform.scale (zombie, (width, height))

scream = pygame.mixer.Sound('scream.wav')

sleep(randrange(5, 15))

scream.play()

screen.blit(zombie, (0,0))

pygame.display.update()

sleep(3)

scream.stop()

pygame.quit()
```

You have now successfully created a game which will give anybody who tries to play it a spooky surprise!

GENERAL TIPS

1. Although indentation is probably the most used function in Python programming, it is also the reason for the program running into an error most of the time. This error is usually a mistake made in the indentation. When looking for problems and fixing them in the code of a program in a

process called debugging, always double-check the indentations before searching for some other causes.

2. Many programming languages use American English spellings, and Python is no exception: the command for changing the color of the turtle's pen is spelled color, and if you spell it the British English way as color, it simply won't work. Variables, though, can have any spelling you like – which is why you're able to call your new variable colors and have Python understand.

3. The key to using variables is to learn the difference between = and ==. Remember: = means 'make this variable equal to this value,' while == means 'check to see if the variable is equal to this value.' Mixing them up is a sure way to end up with a program that doesn't work!

4. Python is a zero-indexed language – meaning it starts counting from 0, not from 1 – which is why your program prints the numbers 0 through 9 rather than 1 through 10. If you wanted to, you could change this behavior by switching the range (10) instruction to range (1, 11) – or any other numbers you like.

5. If your program doesn't run but instead prints a 'syntax error' message to the shell area, there's a mistake somewhere in what you've written. Python needs its instructions to be written in a very specific way: miss a bracket or a quotation mark, spell 'print' wrong or give it a

capital P, or add extra symbols somewhere in the instruction, and it won't run. Try typing the instruction again, and make sure it matches the version in this book before pressing the ENTER key.

Chapter 6

Physical Computing With Python
And Scratch

Coding or computing is not only bound to affecting software. We can use computing capabilities actually to control hardware as well. We all have experienced physical computing at one point or the other in our daily lives, for instance, setting the temperature on the thermostat is an example of physical computing because our interaction with the computer is, in fact, interaction with hardware.

Having the General Purpose Input/Output (GPIO) header, the Raspberry Pi is an excellent guinea pig on which we can experiment with physical computing.

WHAT IS A GPIO HEADER?

The name of this component comes from its purpose. When a component like this is exposed on a circuit, it comes to be known as a header. This component does not have a fixed purpose, so it can be used for a wide range of projects and as an input or output connector, depending on what you want to use it for.

As explained in the very first chapter of this book, the GPIO header is characterized by two long protruding rows of metal pins. This header is located at the top edge of the Raspberry Pi circuit board and can be used to connect various hardware, for example, LEDs (light-emitting diodes)

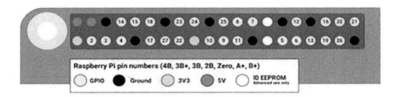

Above is an image of a typical GPIO header you can find on the Raspberry Pi systems. Notice how the pins are grouped so that out of the 40 male pins, you can use only a bunch of them for your physical computing project, and other pins are reserved for various purposes like providing power or communicating with external hardware (for example the Sense HAT).

Below is a table detailing the different types of a pin found on the GPIO header and their respective functions.

3V3	3.3 Volts power	A permanently-on source of 3.3 V power, the same voltage the Raspberry Pi runs at internally
5V	5 Volts power	A permanently-on source of 5 V power, the same voltage as the Raspberry Pi takes in at the

		micro USB power connector
GROUND (GND)	0 Volts ground	A ground connection used to complete a circuit connected to the power source
GPIO XX	General Purpose Input/Output pin number 'XX.'	The GPIO pins available for your programs, identified by a number from 2 to 27
ID EEPROM	Reserved special purpose pins	Pins reserved for use with Hardware Attached on Top (HAT) and other accessories

VARIOUS ELECTRICAL COMPONENTS

We cannot entirely work with the GPIO header to explore physical computing. We need a combination of necessary electrical components and the GPIO header. The electrical components signify the hardware we are going to use, and the GPIO header is the control center that directly controls this external hardware. There's no need to go out and buy complicated circuitry and electrical hardware. Instead, we just need common electrical components for our physical computing project.

1. First is the Breadboard.

2. This particular electrical component is the most commonly used piece of hardware in many of the physical computing projects nowadays because of how convenient it makes connecting the wires of separate components by joining them with the help of metal tracks that are hidden underneath its surface. On the outside, it looks like a simple board, but its true value lies in on what you can use it for. This is why it is also known as a solderless board because you just pop in the wires and connect them instead of soldering them. This particular component is not necessary for our project, but it is very useful, regardless.

3. The second component commonly used in physical computing are jumper wires (or more commonly referred to as jumper leads). Basically, these leads are a substitute for the breadboard because they connect the electrical components to the Raspberry Pi. These jumper leads can be found in three versions depending on the type of wire you are connecting; Male to Male (M2M) make connections from one part of the breadboard to the other, Female to Female (F2F), connect individual components together and Male to Female (M2F), connecting a breadboard to GPIO pins. When using jumper leads with a breadboard, we usually need only M2F and M2M versions.

4. The next component commonly used is a switch. There are a variety of switches that can be used. From the standard push-button switch (the type you'll see in cartoons, a big red

button) or a latching switch (which stays active once toggled and disabled when toggled again).

5. A component that can be used for a variety of purposes in different projects. The LED (light-emitting diode). They come in various shapes, colors, and sizes so you can choose the one which suits your physical computing project the best.

6. One of the essential electrical components in any circuit or electrical project. The Resistor. It basically controls the flow of electricity (electric current) and has different resistance values. So choose the one which you need for your project.

7. The buzzer is an electrical component that produces a buzzing sound. Just as how LEDs produce light, buzzers produce a noise that can be programmed to trigger a certain event when connected to the GPIO header. There are two versions of buzzers, an active buzzer, and a passive buzzer. Active buzzers are more preferred because they are simpler to use.

Below is a list of all the electrical components which we will use for demonstrating some physical computing examples in this chapter.

- 3 LEDs can be red, green, blue, yellow, or amber.

- 2 push button switches

- 1 active buzzer

- 2 Jumper leads, one Male to Female (M2F) and one Female to Female (F2F)

- A breadboard along with Male to Male jumper leads.

CONTROLLING THE LED LIGHT USING PROGRAMMING TOOLS

It's traditional to control the lighting up of an LED as the first step towards learning physical computing (Just as how the first project we learn in programmings such as python or scratch is printing a message such as 'Good Morning).

This project will be controlling the Light Emitting Diode connects to the GPIO header of our Raspberry Pi by using instructions from Scratch.

The components required for this project are; an LED, 330-ohm resistor (or any resistor close to 330 ohm), and a female to female (F2F) jumper leads.

Once we have gathered the required components, the first thing we need to do is connect the LED to our Raspberry Pi and see if it's functional. Connecting an LED is really simple, just follow these steps;

1. Take the resistor and using a female to female jumper wire, connect the resistor to the first 3V3 pin on the GPIO header, then connect the other end of the resistor to the long leg of the LED by using another F2F jumper wire.

2. Take one more female to female jumper wire and connect the short leg (negative cathode) of your LED to the first ground pin on the GPIO header.

3. The wires thus connected should resemble this diagram;

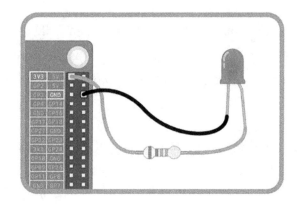

The LED should light up on its own when you turn the power up your Raspberry Pi. If the LED is not lighting up, first check the resistor you used to see if it doesn't have a high resistance value. If that doesn't work, check the pin connections, you might have connected one of the wires to the wrong pin. Also, check if you properly connected the short and long leg of the LED to the proper jumper wire. If the LED lights up, then we proceed to the next step of this project, which is to use Scratch to code a program that will control this LED's behavior. But before that, remember to disconnect the jumper wire, which is currently connected to the 3V3 pin and switch it over to the GP25 Pin (this will turn the LED off, that's normal).

The wire connection should look like this;

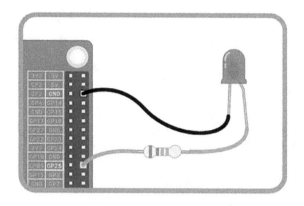

We can move towards coding a program that will turn our LED on or OFF.

USING SCRATCH TO PROGRAM AN LED CONTROLLER

Open up the Scratch 2 application. Before we drag any blocks, we first need to import blocks that are made to be used with the Pi's GPIO. To do this, go to the blocks palette and over there, find and click the 'More Blocks' option followed by the 'Add an extension' button. You'll see a window with two circuits, select the 'Pi GPIO' option, and click OK. The blocks palette will now load all the blocks which are needed for controlling the GPIO header of Raspberry Pi.

Now that we have access to the blocks we need, follow the steps detailed below;

1. Drag the event trigger block 'when clicked' onto the scripts area.

2. Find the 'set gpio to output high' block and place it beneath the trigger block. On this block, open the dropdown list by clicking on the small arrow and specify the pin you're using on the GPIO; in our case, we are using the GPIO 25 pin.

3. We have now programmed the 'turn on' command for the LED. Check it out by clicking the green flag icon; the LED will stay on. Now we will add more blocks, a forever loop block, two 'wait for 1 secs' blocks, and another 'set gpio output high' block. But this time, change the output of the second GPIO block to low.

We have now created a program that turns our LED off and on after every second until we manually terminate the program from Scratch. Play with this sequence of the block to make your LED sleep for longer or stay on for longer and experiment how you can add more blocks to change the LED's behavior.

USING PYTHON TO PROGRAM AN LED CONTROLLER

Close the Scratch application and fire up Thonny Python IDE. We will now use python to code a program that will turn our LED on or off.

Click the start of a new project icon, give it any name you want and follow the steps outlined below;

1. Before we can code a program that is aimed at the GPIO pins, we first need to import a library into Python. The library we will be importing is GPIO Zero; however, for this

project, we only require a portion of this library, not the complete library. Starting off, type in the following code;

from gpiozero import LED

2. Now, we will tell the computer which pins on the GPIO header is our LED connected to.

led = LED(25)

3. Add the lines of code which directly control the output state of the LED (on or off).

led.on()

led.off()

4. We will turn these simple set of instructions into a true program which will turn the LED on or off depending on its current state with a sleep delay of 1 second.

from gpiozero import LED

from time import sleep

led = LED(25)

while True:

  led.on()

    sleep(1)

led.off()

sleep(1)

EXPLANATION

Using python, we have just created a program that turns the LED on or off with a 1-second delay between each cycle. This change in the LED's output state is infinite because we have not specified a stop condition in the code. Moreover, in the beginning, we imported the GPIO Zero and Time library so we could use the LED and sleep function, respectively.

USE OF A BREADBOARD

A breadboard is primarily used to hold down multiple electrical hardware components to make electrical connections.

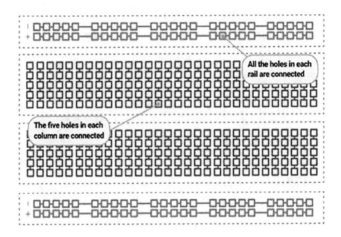

If you look at the diagram above, you'll see an x-ray demonstration of how many holes a breadboard has. These holes are either connected to each other vertically or horizontally. Underneath holes, you'll find metal strips. These act as a substitute for the jumper leads (or wires), which we have been using to connect components together until now.

Looking at the above image, you'll probably get the notion that using a breadboard and connecting the wires of electrical components is a really complicated procedure, but in reality, it's quite the opposite. Connecting different electrical components together is very simple; all you need to do is line up the head (the sticky metal parts) of the component which you want to connect into the breadboard and give it a gentle push until it goes into place. To make connections, you will need to use Male to Male (M2M) jumper wires to connect a wire to the breadboard and use a Female to Male (F2M) jumper wire to connect the breadboard to the Raspberry Pi.

CODE FOR READING THE BUTTON INPUT USING SCRATCH

Until now, we have focused on the 'Output' part of the GPIO header. In this project, we will focus on the 'Input' part. Input on a GPIO header means that we can use the GPIO pins as input.

The components required for this project are; A breadboard, Male to Male jumper wires, Male to Female jumper wires, a push-button switch.

Before we can go to Scratch and code a controlling program for a button, we first need to connect the button to the breadboard. A switch can have four legs or two legs. If the switch you are using only has two legs, make sure that each leg is in a different numbered row on the breadboard. Connect the ground rail of your breadboard to a ground pin of the Raspberry Pi (marked GND) with a male-to-female jumper wire, then connect one leg of your push-button to the ground rail with a male-to-male jumper wire. Finally, connect the other leg (the one on the same side as the leg you just connected) if using a four-leg switch to the GPIO 2 pin (marked GP2) of the Raspberry Pi with a male-to-female jumper wire.

The assembly of the components should look like this;

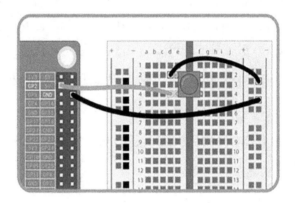

Now we can finally hop on to Scratch and start coding for reading the button. Open the Scratch application, start a new project and follow the steps below;

- Drag the 'when clicked' event trigger block into the scripts area

- Drag the 'set gpio output high' block and place it underneath the event trigger block

- On the 'set gpio output high' block, set the pin number to 2, and at the end of the block, change the mode from output to input. (Clicking the green flag icon to trigger the event right now will do nothing because we have not yet told the computer what to do with the input)

- Drag a 'forever' loop block and a conditional 'if then else' block from the Controls category of the blocks palette and place it beneath the 'set gpio 2 to input' block.

- From the blocks palette, find the 'gpio is high?' diamond-shaped block and place it inside the conditional block. The pin number being used it 2, so specify it in the gpio blocks accordingly.

- From the blocks palette, find the 'say hello for 2 secs' block and drop it in the 'else' part of the 'if then else' conditional block. Modify the message in the 'say hello for 2 secs' block to 'say Button pushed! For 2 secs.' (Try to test this program. First, click the trigger icon to start the program. Once that is done, go to the breadboard and push the button. If everything has been set up correctly up to this point, then the program should display the message 'Button Pushed.' If you see this message displayed by the sprite in Scratch, then your program has successfully read input from the GPIO header)

(Notice how the if part of the block is not being followed up by any code. The code which is executed when the button is pushed in the else part of the block instead of the 'if' part of the block. This is because the GPIO input pins on the Raspberry Pi are in a 'high' or 'on' state by default, and pressing the button offsets this state to 'low.' This is why the program notices that the gpio pin state is low and skips over to the 'else' part of the code)

1. Although we have successfully made the Raspberry Pi read the input from the button, we can further extend this project by including the previous project (LED and Resistor) into the current setup. Connect the LED's long leg (attached to the resistor) to GPIO pin 25 and the short leg to the ground rail of the breadboard.

2. Replace the 'say Button pushed! for 2 secs' with a 'set gpio 25 to output high' block (you'll have to edit the default block to this configuration).

3. Once again, add the 'set gpio 25 to output high' block but this time in the empty space of the 'if' part of the conditional block. After adding this block, change the output state from 'high' to 'low.'

The code is now complete.

RESULT

When you activate the program by pressing the event trigger icon (green flag) and proceed to push the button, the LED, which we added, will light up and will remain turned on as long as the button is pushed down. We are now controlling a GPIO pin from the input on another GPIO pin. Pretty neat.

CODE FOR READING THE BUTTON INPUT USING PYTHON

First, close Scratch and open up Thonny Python IDE from the Raspberry Pi menu. Start a new project and save it with any name you like. Last time, we used the GPIO Zero Library, but this time we will be importing a different part of this library into python for our project. Start off by typing the following line of code;

from gpiozero import Button

button = Button(2)

By importing the button function from the GPIO Zero library, we can use the wait_for_press function to instruct the program to halt further action until an input is received.

button.wait_for_press()

print("You pushed me!")

That's it! As soon as you press the button, the message will be displayed in the python shell area. As there's no loop in this program, you'll have to run the program again manually if and then press the button to get an output on the python shell area window again. As the LED project has already been set up with the breadboard, we will also extend the code to encompass these components.

Just like before, import the LED function from the GPIO Zero library and the sleep function from the Time library and type in the following lines of code at the top of the script area as the new initial lines of code;

from gpiozero import LED

from time import sleep

Type in the following line of code underneath **button = Button(2)**

led = LED(25)

replace the line print("you pushed me!") with the following lines of code

led.on()

sleep(3)

led.off()

The sequence of the entire code will be;

from gpiozero import LED

from time import sleep

from gpiozero import Button

button = Button(2)

led = LED(25)

button.wait_for_press()

led.on()

sleep(3)

led.off()

Run the program and then push the button on the breadboard. You'll see that as soon as you press the button, the LED turns on for 3 seconds before going dim. We have successfully programmed the GPIO to take in an input and give an output at the same time.

PYTHON PROJECT: INSTANT RESPONSE GAME

Let's put all of our knowledge we learned so far about physical computing into making a game that will test the reaction time of the players to see who's the fastest.

The components required for this project are;

1. One breadboard

2. One LED

3. 330-ohm resistor

4. Two push-button switches

5. A bunch of Male to Female (M2F) jumper wires

6. A bunch of Male to Male (M2M) jumper wires

Once we have gathered all the components, we need to assemble them like this;

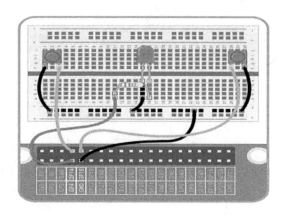

Fire up the Thonny Python IDE application from the Raspberry Pi menu, click the new project and save it with the name **Instant Response Game**.

As you can see in the above diagram, we are using buttons and an LED, hence we in python, we will import the LED and Button functions from the GPIO Zero library along with the Sleep function from the Time library.

from gpiozero import LED, Button

from time import sleep

After importing the required functions from the GPIO Zero library, we need to specify the GPIO pins connected to the external components in the Python code.

led = LED(4)

right_button = Button(15)

left_button = Button(14)

Now the program knows where the buttons and pins are located on the GPIO header. Time to add in some instructions

led.on()

sleep(5)

led.off()

However, the blinking of the LED is too predictable; let's add a bit randomness. Go to the top of the script and add in the following lines importing the functions;

from random import uniform

Now we can add the unpredictable factor to the blinking of the LED. Replace the line **sleep(5)** with the following line of code

sleep(uniform(5, 10))

Now when the program is executed, the LED will blink for a random period, anywhere between 5 to 10 seconds. Now to add the element of a game to the project.

Since we have two buttons each, we will turn them into triggers, which will light up the LED as soon as they are pressed. Continue the code and the following lines

def pressed(button):

   print(str(button.pin.number) + "won the game")

right_button.when_pressed = pressed

left_button.when_pressed = pressed

We will now assign names to each individual button, which will serve as the player name. We will ask the players for their names at the beginning of the game, so add the following lines of code below the **from random import uniform** line of code

left_name = input("Left player's name is ")

right_name = input("Right player's name is ")

Now navigate back to the function and program the win condition of the game

if button.pin.number == 14

    print(left_name + "won the game")

else:

    print(right_name + "won the game")

However, there's still one problem with the game; the program reports all of the button presses as having won, so to remedy this, we will use another function imported from the sys library. Type this line under the last import function line

from os import_exit

Type the following line of code under the line **print(right_name +
"won the game")**

_exit(0)

This specific instruction tells the Python to terminate the program
as soon the first button is pressed. This will stop the button press of
the losing player to be registered as having won the game.

The final sequence of the program should look like this;

from gpiozero import LED, Button

from time import sleep

from random import uniform

from os import _exit

left_name = input("Left player name is ")

right_name = input ("Right player name is ")

led = LED(4)

right_button = Button(15)

left_button = Button(14)

led.on()

sleep(uniform(5, 10))

```python
    led.off()


def pressed(button):
    if button.pin.number == 14:
            print(left_name + " won the game")
    else:
            print(right_name + " won the game")
    _exit(0)

right_button.when_pressed = pressed

left_button.when_pressed = pressed
```

Chapter 7

Trying Out Projects Using Sense Hat Emulator

WHAT IS A SENSE HAT?

By now, it is no surprise that this tiny device packs a lot of features and capabilities that you would normally find on a full-sized desktop Personal Computer. However, we have still not reached the limits of what the Raspberry Pi is capable of. You'll be surprised to find out that this credit-card-sized computer is even being used for projects in the Astro Pi space mission!

This suitability for computation and carrying out projects in such environments is because of a special hardware add-on support in the Raspberry Pi, to be specific, the Sense HAT. HAT's are basically known as Hardware Attached on Top. Just as the name suggests, a wide range of hardware ranging from microphones, lights to electronic relays, and screens can be added on top of the Raspberry Pi. But out of all these add-on's, one stands out from the rest; the Sense HAT. This hardware add-on was designed and made specifically for the Astro Pi space mission (which is actually a joint project featuring the collaboration of the Raspberry Pi Foundation UK, UK Space Agency, and European Space Agency).

This Sense HAT is primarily used in the Astro Pi space mission to run code and carry out scientific experiments contributed by school children from all over Europe.

Although the Sense HAT being used in the space mission is out of our reach, but luckily, the same hardware is available on our big blue marble at all Raspberry Pi retailers to grab and experiment on.

However, in this chapter, we will be focusing on running our projects through the Sense HAT emulator, as working with the real Sense HAT is an advanced topic. Hence it will be addressed in the next book of this series. But don't worry, the emulator works just as good as the real thing

THE COMPONENTS OF THE SENSE HAT

On the surface, the Sense HAT is made up of a programmable 8x8 64 matrix LED, which supports the entire RGB spectrum, being able to produce and display any color from a range of millions. Apart from this, the hardware add-on has a five-way joystick controller and six on-board sensors.

Here's an illustration of what a typical Sense HAT looks like:

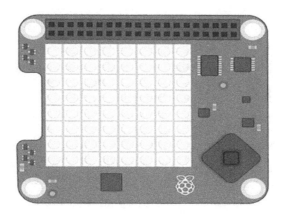

The six sensors included in the Sense HAT are:

1. The Gyroscope: this sensor detects changes in the angle of the hardware in which it is mounted on by keeping track of the Earth's directional magnetic field and comparing it with the angular velocity of the device. Hence, this sensor is capable of displaying information such as notifying when the Sense HAT is being rotated relative to the surface of the Earth and how fast it is rotating.

2. The Accelerometer: this sensor is somewhat similar to a gyroscope in a sense that instead of measuring the current angle relative to the Earth's gravity, it measures acceleration force in multiple directions. When the gyroscope and accelerometer are combined, the composite data can be manipulated to find out where the Sense HAT is pointing to and how it is being moved.

3. The Magnetometer: is another sensor that can be used to find out the direction of the Sense HAT. The magnetometer basically calculates the position of the Earth's magnetic pole

relative to its current position. Aside from measuring the Earth's natural magnetic field, the magnetometer is also capable of detecting electrical fields and metallic objects. All three of these sensors are found on the same chip, which is labeled 'ACCEL/GYRO/MAG' on the circuit board of the Sense HAT.

4. The Humidity Sensor: just as the name suggests, this sensor detects the relative humidity of the immediate atmosphere by measuring the number of water vapors in the air. This data can be used to predict when it will rain.

5. The Barometric pressure sensor: does the same job a traditional barometer would do, measuring the air pressure, but with more accuracy. Since this sensor can determine the air pressure, it can also detect when you're going uphill or downhill because the air pressure changes based on height.

6. The Temperature sensor: is a kind of a thermometer. It measures the temperature of its immediate surroundings. But this is not really reliable as the measured readings are also influenced by hot the Sense HAT also is and will also factor in the temperature of the Raspberry Pi (if you're using an enclosed case).

SENSE HAT PYTHON PROJECTS

Now that we know what are the major components of the Sense HAT let us move on to code a program that will make use of its mounted matrix LED.

The Sense HAT emulator can be accessed from the web browser using the following URL https://www.raspberrypi.org/blog/sense-hat-emulator/

When you type in and run code on this emulator, you'll be redirected to a Sense HAT visualizer which will virtually depict the instructions of your program

SAYING HELLO

Before we can type in instructions for the Sense HAT emulator, we first need to import some functions from the **sense_emu** library. Type the following lines of code in the scripts area of the trinket Sense HAT emulator.

from sense_emu import SenseHat

sense = SenseHat()

sense.show_message("This is really cool!")

After typing in the following instructions, click the run button (a play icon), and the emulator will simulate the instructions on a virtual Sense HAT, displaying this message on the matrix LED.

However, the show_message() function is not as bland as we made it out to be; in fact, it has a lot of tricks up its sleeve that we can use in our code. For instance, go back to the scripts area by clicking the pencil icon on top and edit the last line of the code;

sense.show_message("This is really cool!" text_color=(255, 255, 0), back_color=(0, 0, 255), scroll_speed=(0.05))

All of this extra instruction we have just added into the show_message() function is commonly referred to as parameters. These parameters are responsible for controlling various aspects of the show_message function.

The text_color=() and black_color=() parameters basically determine and specify the color of the writing and the background of the lighting of the Matrix display, respectively. If you look into the color parameter, it has three values each. This is because every parameter needs input for the prime colors (Red, Green, and Blue, hence known as RGB). The first parameter is for Red, the second for Green and the third parameter is for the color Blue. If we look at the text_color=(255, 255, 0) parameter, it specifies maximum red (255), maximum green (255), and no blue at all (0).

Similarly, one of the basic parameters in the show.message() function is the scroll_speed parameter. The purpose is exactly as the name suggests; it controls the speed of the text scrolling through the matrix display of the Sense HAT. The bigger the input number of the parameter, the slower the scroll speed of the text. The value 0.05 in this parameter change's the speed of the text to twice of the original.

Click the run button and notice how differently the same message is being displayed. You can also play with these parameters to change the color and speed to find the right combination that is to your liking.

We can also assign variables to a color parameter that we created in the RGB spectrum. To do this, assign a name to a color followed by an equal sign and the parameter, which represents that specific color. Remember to define these variables before the **sense.show_message()** function, or they won't work. For example;

yellow = (255, 255, 0)

blue = (0, 0, 255)

Now we can use these variables instead of the color parameters.

sense.show_message("This is really cool!", text_color=(yellow), back_color=(blue), scroll_speed=(0.05))

If you run the program now, you'll notice that nothing has changed on the Matrix Display. This confirms that the variables are working. To add the white color, you need to use the parameter (255, 255, 255), and to add the black color, you will need to use the following variable (0, 0, 0).

We can also display individual letters on the screen. But to do this, we will not use the sense.show_message() function but instead we will use another more suitable function;

sense.show_letter("Z")

Individual letters do not scroll, and hence, they stay on the display. We can play with the letter's color and the background color, to do this, just use the same parameters used in the sense.show_message() parameter.

DRAWING A PICTURE ON THE MATRIX LED

Moving on to the next project, click the 'plus' icon on the right side to start coding for a new program. In this project, we will be using the RGB lights of the Sense HAT matrix display to draw the face of a Minecraft character, a creeper!

Start by importing the SenseHat function from the sense_emu library.

from sense_emu import SenseHat

sense = SenseHat()

sense.clear(255, 255, 255)

If you run the program now, the virtual Sense HAT will be showing a bright white color on its display.

This sense.clear() function is used to clear the LEDs of any previous programming giving us a clean slate to work on now. Let's try changing the LED matrix display's color from white to green

sense.clear(0, 255, 0)

Run the program, and you'll see that the entire display of the Sense HAT has turned green. You can now experiment with different colors and associate colors with variables to use later in coding.

After you're done playing with the colors, you can clear the led by just typing in

sense.clear()

This will turn the color of the entire matrix display to black (the display will go dark, in other words, switch off). Whenever you want to clear the matrix display completely, this is the easiest way to do so.

We will now proceed to create a portrait of a creeper on the LED matrix display. To create our own version of the LED matrix pixels lighting up (specific pixels on the matrix lighting up instead of the whole display), use the following lines of code after clearing the display

sense.clear()

sense.set_pixel(0, 2, (0, 0, 255))

sense.set_pixel(7, 4, (255, 0, 0))

In the above lines of code, the first two numbers in the round brackets specify the position of the pixels on the matrix display while the following numbers are parameters specifying the color for that pixel. The first number is the position of the pixel along the X (horizontal) axis and the second number is the position of the pixel along the Y (vertical) axis. Run the program and you'll see that the virtual Sense HAT's display lights up only at 2 points. This was just to demonstrate how to light up specific pixels, delete these lines and type in the following code

sense.set_pixel(2, 2, (0, 0, 255))

sense.set_pixel(4, 2, (0, 0, 255))

sense.set_pixel(3, 4, (100, 0, 0))

sense.set_pixel(1, 5, (255, 0, 0))

sense.set_pixel(2, 6, (255, 0, 0))

sense.set_pixel(3, 6, (255, 0, 0))

sense.set_pixel(4, 6, (255, 0, 0))

sense.set_pixel(5, 5, (255, 0, 0))

You can find out the coordinates of the pixels detailed above by drawing an 8x8 matrix and labeling the position of each pixel in that matrix horizontally and vertically.

However, detailing an entire portrait out of the set_pixel function is a really slow process. However, there is a way to speed up the process, delete all the set_pixel lines of code and replace them with the following;

g = (0, 255, 0)

```
b = (0, 0, 0)

creeper_pixels = [

g, g, g, g, g, g, g, g,

g, g, g, g, g, g, g, g,

g, b, b, g, g, b, b, g,

g, b, b, g, g, b, b, g,

g, g, g, b, b, g, g, g,

g, g, b, b, b, b, g, g,

g, g, b, b, b, b, g, g,

g, g, b, g, g, b, g, g

]


sense.set_pixels(creeper_pixels)
```

There are a lot of characters in this code, but first off, run the program and see if you can recognize a creepy creeper! We have accelerated the coding and execution process and also made it easier to write at the same time, all by defining the colors which we want to use by variables and using these variables to define a block representing the Sense HAT display's entire pixel count.

Now all we need to do is use this variable **creeper_pixels** with the **sense.set_pixel()** function, and we are done!

We can also animate the portrait on the Sense Hat display by adding the following line of code onto the start of our program;

from time import sleep

After importing library, go to the bottom of the script and add the following lines of code

while True:

    sleep(1)

    sense.flip_h()

If we run the program now, you will see that the creeper is winking at you!

The flip_h() function flips an image on the horizontal axis, across; if you want to flip an image on its vertical axis, replace sense.flip_h() with sense.flip_v() instead. You can also rotate an image by 0, 90, 180, or 270 degrees using sense.set_rotation(90), changing the number according to how many degrees you want to rotate the image.

ENVIRONMENTAL SENSING

Pressure sensing

In this project, we will make use of the in-built sensors of the Sense HAT. Using a Sense HAT emulator doesn't make this project any different than using a real Sense HAT. The main purpose remains unchanged, and that is to take readings from the sensors.

To start off, clear the script area in the window main.py of the emulator and as usual, import the SenseHat portion of the sense_emu library.

from sense_emu import SenseHat

sense = SenseHat()

sense.clear()

Using the sense.clear() function whenever you start a new Sense HAT project is a good habit because sometimes, the matrix display is still showing something from the previous program, although you cleared the script. So remember always to use the sense.clear() function when starting a new code or re-writing the display.

First, let's take a reading from the pressure sensor of the Sense HAT. To do this, use the following lines of code;

pressure = sense.get_pressure()

print(pressure)

As you can see, we have first assigned the sense_get.pressure() a variable making it easier to use in future lines of code in the same program. Then we just used the print function **print(pressure)** to display the pressure reading. The reading you will obtain from the Sense HAT's barometer will be in millibars, and if you are working with a Real Sense HAT, then you can try blowing on the add-on and you'll see that the reading this time around is higher than before.

You can also change the values reported on the Sense HAT emulator by using the sliders and buttons of each of the emulated sensors. Go ahead and try sliding the pressure setting of the Sense HAT down by a notch and run the program again. You'll notice a difference in the readings.

Humidity sensing

Now let's switch to the humidity sensor and display its measured readings. The code structure is very similar, just remove the last two lines in the script area that we wrote for the pressure sensor and replace them with;

humidity = sense.get_humidity()

print(humidity)

Run the program, and you'll notice another type of reading. This is the current virtual humidity of the emulated Sense HAT. You can check it out by moving the humidity slider of the emulator up or down and see if the reading changes by running the program again.

Temperature sensing

Same procedure as the last one, just replace the last two lines of code in the scripts area of the current program with;

temp = sense.get_temperature()

print(temp)

Run the program, and you'll see an output displaying the emulator Sense HAT's current temperature in degrees Celcius. Usually, the temperature reading is actually obtained from the humidity sensor but you can also get the temperature reading from the pressure sensor as well. To do this, use the following line of code;

htemp = sense.get_temperature()

ptemp = sense.get_temperature_from_pressure()

temp = (htemp + ptemp) / 2

print(temp)

This time, the reading obtained from the code will be based on the readings from both the sensors instead of a single one (an average reading from both, which is why we divided the measurement by 2). However, this is only applicable for an actual Sense HAT, because the emulated Sense HAT's humidity, pressure, and the average will yield the same result.

Inertial sensing

This is the last method we will need to learn because it covers both the magnetometer, the gyroscope, and the accelerometer.

To use information from the IMU to determine the current orientation of the device in 3 axes, use;

from sense_emu import SenseHat

```
sense = SenseHat()

sense.clear()

orientation = sense.get_orientation()

pitch = orientation["pitch"]

roll = orientation["roll"]

yaw = orientation["yaw"]

print("pitch {0} roll {1} yaw {2}".format(pitch, roll, yaw))
```

Run the program and you will be given readings detailing the virtual Sense HAT's orientation according to the three axis (x axis, y axis and z axis).

To detect movement, delete all the lines of code after sense.clear() and add the following lines;

```
while True:

 acceleration = sense.get_accelerometer_raw()

 x = acceleration['x']

 y = acceleration['y']

 z = acceleration['z']

 x = round(x)
```

```python
y = round(y)

z = round(z)

print("x={0}, y={1}, z={2}".format(x, y, z))
```

The following program will print values from the accelerometer to the python shell area.

Conclusion

This is the end of the adventure for beginners covering the Realms of the Raspberry Pi.

We started from the simplest of concepts and learned the details of the hardware components of the Raspberry Pi. After laying a foundation to understanding how similar the Raspberry Pi system is to a traditional desktop PC, we learned how to set up our Raspberry Pi's hardware and installed our first OS on it.

After getting to know the in's and out's of the Raspberry Pi's hardware and software, we became ready to take the next step in the world of computers and learned the basics of programming. We learned about the Pi's visual and interactive Scratch programming language and also included today's popular Python programming so that we can benefit from the best of both worlds.

Then we end the journey of learning about the Raspberry Pi by finishing off with the world of Physical computing and delving into its basics whilst incorporating the newly learned knowledge in a few interactive examples. In this book, we learned a lot so that we may be prepared to take part in projects involving the Raspberry Pi or possibly even design our own.

The Raspberry Pi is indeed a technological marvel, and it will always be amazing as to what this tiny machine is capable of. Not only does this little monster pack a punch in terms of power and capability, but the Raspberry Pi is also in a league of its own with regards to its adaptability to an entire array of possible applications. Just as how the Raspberry Pi's usefulness knows no limits and has no defined boundary, we could only learn so much in this beginner's level book. There's still an entire island's worth of knowledge to still explore regarding the Pi and its capability and how we can use it to the best of its abilities. However, this book has addressed all of the essential concepts to their basic form so that the reader will be able to tackle any problem he comes across if he wants to use the Raspberry Pi as a pocket computer or as a project piece.

In short, the Raspberry Pi is a small circuit board capable of big things. Learning about it requires proper guidance, and so far, we have addressed that job to the best of our abilities. The next book in the Raspberry Pi guide series will address some new concepts and also prove to be an extension to the concepts detailed in this book by taking such concepts to the next level of understanding

www.ingramcontent.com/pod-product-compliance
Lightning Source LLC
LaVergne TN
LVHW051242050326
832903LV00028B/2535